Native Plant GARDENING FOR BIRDS, BEES & BUTTERFLIES

Northern California

George Oxford Miller

Adventure Publications
Cambridge, Minnesota

DEDICATION

Dedicated to my birth father, George Oxford, known to many in the Bay area as Jumpin' George for spinning Rhythm & Blues for 40 years on KSAN-AM and KDIA-AM.

ACKNOWLEDGMENTS

This book is but one additional step built on the decades-long efforts of numerous individuals and organizations who champion landscaping with native plants to remediate the environmental damage caused by human development.

O Friend!

In the garden of thy heart plant naught but the rose of love.

—Bahá'u'lláh, founder of the Bahá'í Faith

Cover and book design by Jonathan Norberg
Edited by Brett Ortler and Ritchey Halphen
Proofread by Dan Downing

All cover photos by George Oxford Miller unless otherwise noted.
(Front cover) Twinberry: **Peter Turner Photograpy/shutterstock.com;** background for hummingbird: **Stephen Whybrow/shutterstock.com;** Allen's Hummingbird: **Keneva Photography/shutterstock.com;** Checkered White butterfly: **Sari ONeal/shutterstock.com**
(Back cover) This image is licensed under the Attribution 2.0 Generic (CC BY 2.0) license, which is available at https://creativecommons.org/licenses/by/2.0/: **Colin Durfee:** Twice-stabbed Lady Beetle on California Fescue, no modifications, original image at https://www.flickr.com/photos/146003125@N02/49912004107/

10 9 8 7 6 5 4 3 2 1
Native Plant Gardening for Birds, Bees & Butterflies: Northern California
Copyright © 2022 by George Oxford Miller
Published by Adventure Publications
An imprint of AdventureKEEN
310 Garfield Street South
Cambridge, Minnesota 55008
(800) 678-7006
www.adventurepublications.net
All rights reserved
Printed in the United States of America
ISBN 978-1-64755-255-8 (pbk.); ISBN 978-1-64755-256-5 (ebook)

Table of Contents

Introduction

In 2008, when I published my book about landscaping with native plants of Southern California, climate change, reoccurring mega-wildfires, the 1,000-year drought engulfing the West, and the global "insect apocalypse" were possible regional concerns but largely ignored in the press, politics, and the national and global conversations. Now old voices and new paradigms are coming to the forefront. In California, a century of efforts by advocates for native plant landscaping, starting in 1915 with Theodore Payne's first demonstration garden in Los Angeles, has exhibited the intrinsic beauty, landscape adaptability, and low-maintenance values of native species over thirsty exotics from a water standpoint. Native plant landscaping has emerged as a cornerstone issue for public water policy, budgets, and lifestyles—and now, more than ever, of conscience.

The first two decades of the 21st century have witnessed an alarming increase in environmental destruction caused by urban sprawl, industrial expansion, global-scale pollution, and planet-wide climate change. In Northern California, population density in the Bay Area (18,832 people per square mile in 2021) is the highest in the state and second only to New York City. Besides sacrificing native habitat to the greatest urban sprawl in the nation, California also loses millions of acres each year to super-droughts and mega-wildfires. Pollinators around the world have been hit particularly hard, with some regions losing up to 80% of their insect numbers and diversity. From farmlands to virgin rainforests, the broken food chain has decreased bird numbers by up to 50% and California Monarch Butterflies in the Central Coast overwintering groves by 99%. Now, a major emphasis in native plant landscaping is to mitigate the habitat lost due to human activity and climate change. A pollinator garden that restores native habitat will help repair our local environment one yard at a time.

Why Plant a Pollinator Garden?

The complex relationships in nature can fill us with a deep sense of mystery and awe. You can look into the starry night sky and either feel insignificant in the scope of the universe or thrill at being a part of the vast majestic cosmos. You can get the same feeling in your backyard when you see a butterfly or bee dancing from flower to flower, sipping nectar and gathering pollen. When you see a butterfly perched on a flower, you get a glimpse into an evolutionary pathway that stretches back unbroken for 150 million years.

From our backyards to the tropical rainforests, the intricate web that sustains life on the planet depends on native pollinators. Globally, insects pollinate nearly 80% of all flowering plants. Closer to home, pollinators fertilize one-third of all human food crops—the fruit, vegetables, and nuts we eat (grains are wind pollinated). In our backyard gardens, tomatoes, squash, peppers, fruit trees, and flowers all depend on pollinators.

Yet across the planet, the population of all insects is plummeting radically year by year. One overriding reason is that human activities have significantly altered 75% of the planet's landmass. Within the continental United States, 40% of the natural area has been altered, including 75% of the original vegetation in the California Floristic Province. With the state's burgeoning population, pristine plant and animal communities that have evolved together since the last ice age have been replaced by sprawling cities, suburbs, industrialized farms, and energy development.

A significant portion of the natural habitat sacrificed for urban expansion has been replaced by homes, businesses, and public medians and roadsides that are landscaped with gravel and exotic ornamentals imported from other parts of the world. For native pollinators, such landscapes offer about as much sustenance as an asphalt parking lot. The simple fact is that native pollinators need native plants to survive.

What good will a small backyard garden do to help sustain local pollinator populations? You will be pleasantly surprised! Wildlife in California's coastal sage scrub, chaparral, valley grasslands, and deserts live in what ecologists call a "patchy environment." Butterflies, bees, birds, and other pollinators forage over large areas, depending on their mobility, to find often ephemeral patches of food, water, shelter, and nesting sites.

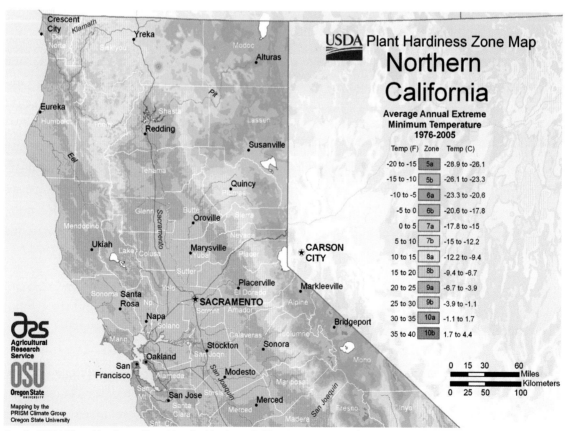

Credit: *USDA Plant Hardiness Zone Map for Northern California,* 2012. Agricultural Research Service, US Department of Agriculture. Accessed from planthardiness.ars.usda.gov.

Many of the temporary oases that pollinators frequent on their daily foraging routes are no larger than the average backyard. But our yards can be more than a here-today, gone-tomorrow stopover. The greater gardening goal goes beyond planting a patch of pretty flowers, though that's certainly commendable in itself. It encompasses the long-term development of a mini backyard refuge—a wildlife habitat that supplies the food, water, shelter, and nesting sites that butterflies, bees, and birds require to support a year-round sustainable population.

Gardens start with a dream and build into a passion. This book will help you create a pollinator garden encompassing a diversity of plants with a variety of sizes and shapes, with plants that bloom nearly year-round. So, literally, grab your spade—"plant it and they will come."

A garden in Napa

GARDENING IN THE CALIFORNIA FLORISTIC PROVINCE

Designing and maintaining a pollinator garden—or any type of garden, for that matter—in Central and Northern California requires considerations that are unnecessary in other areas. In this region, which stretches north from San Luis Obispo to the Bay Delta, North Coast, and Oregon, and east across the Coastal Ranges, the Central Valley, and the Sierra Nevada, one size does *not* fit all. The drastically different climates and topography create some of the greatest plant and animal biodiversity on the continent.

Most of California is classified as the California Floristic Province (CFP). The region extends from southern Oregon to Baja California, excluding the Modoc Plateau and deserts, and has a Mediterranean-type climate. This unique climate pattern consists of cool, wet winters and either cool, dry summers (coastal) or hot, dry summers (inland), and it exists in only five places on the planet. The CFP harbors an amazing 3,488 species of vascular plants, of which 2,124, or 61%, are endemic—that is, they occur nowhere else in the world. With so many species and endemics, of both plants and animals, the CFP is considered one of 36 biodiversity hotspots around the world.

In Northern California, the CFP includes 10 ecological regions, including the Northern Coast and ranges, the Central Valley grasslands, the Sierra Nevada range and its foothills, and the Central Coast sage scrub and mountains. Each area contains major vegetative communities and plant associations. Some exist as mosaics that have been severely affected—or eradicated—by agriculture, urbanization, and the introduction of invasive annual grasses and exotics. The San Francisco and Monterey Bays and their associated estuaries are part of the rich marine biome. (Native plants adapted to montane and subalpine conifer forests in low-population areas are not covered in this book. The desert regions are covered in the companion to this book, *Native Plant Gardening for Birds, Bees & Butterflies: Southern California.*)

PLANT COMMUNITIES OF NORTHERN CALIFORNIA

Northern Coastal Sage Scrub 12–25 inches precipitation/year

This semiarid plant community occurs below 3,000 feet along the coast from San Francisco to Monterey. The characteristic plants, mostly 3- to 4-foot-tall shrubs with soft, aromatic leaves, develop shallow roots in thin, rocky soil and depend on seasonal surface moisture for water. Using a drought-deciduous strategy, they cope with the six-month-long summer drought by shedding their leaves and going dormant to conserve energy until the winter rains. Their growing and flowering seasons extend through winter and spring into summer. Many of these plants make ideal drought-tolerant garden selections, providing a burst of winter color and pollinator forage. Dominant species include California Sagebrush, Purple Sage, White Sage, California Buckwheat, Coyote Brush, Bush Monkeyflower, and ceanothus and manzanita species. Winter temperatures may drop to freezing, and mild summers occasionally reach 100°F, with fog and overcast days common. The northern coastal sage scrub community intergrades at higher elevations with chaparral (see below).

Northern Coastal Scrub and Prairie 25–70 inches precipitation/year

Stretching from San Luis Obispo to Oregon, this subset of the coastal sage scrub community is one of the major floristic regions of the Coast Ranges. Dominated by Coyote Brush instead of sages, it consists of prairies in deep, alluvial soils and scrub brushlands on thinner soils of slopes and ravines. It thrives below 1,600 feet in the cool-moist Mediterranean zone between the beach and coastal redwood forests in the north and foothill woodlands in the Central Coast ranges; it also extends east into the Sacramento River delta. Scrub vegetation and prairies often form a mosaic. Dominant plants include Coyote Brush, California Coffeeberry, Blueblossom, Ceanothus, Coast Buckwheat, Seaside Daisy, Giant Coreopsis, Bush Monkeyflower, Salal, and Coastal Yellow Yarrow—all high-value plants for pollinator habitat gardens.

Chaparral 12–30 inches precipitation/year

As the most widespread plant community in California, chaparral occurs on dry, shallow soils in the foothills of the Central Coast to the Sierra foothills. It corresponds to regions with the Mediterranean climate. In native chaparral, densely branched shrubs 4–8 feet tall form impenetrable thickets. When surface moisture is absent, deep taproots reach water trapped in the soil and allow the small, hard evergreen leaves to photosynthesize year-round. Cooler, north-facing slopes may have 5–10 species with none dominating, while arid, sun-baked, south-facing slopes may be dominated by only one species, often Chamise (*Adenostoma fasciculatum*). Many of the evergreen shrubs, such as ceanothus and manzanita species, shrub oaks, sumacs, Toyon, and California Flannel Bush, make premier landscape selections. Winters are moist and usually mild, with occasional hard freezes. Hot, dry summers often reach 100°F. With deeper soil, chaparral transitions into oak woodlands (see below).

California Oak Woodlands 15–35 inches precipitation/year

Also called the valley and foothill woodlands, this zone in Central and Northern California extends through rolling hills and valleys, from 300–2,000 feet on the coast through the northern mountain ranges and around the edges and foothills of the Central Valley. Dominated by several oak species, this plant community varies from savanna to continuous forest, depending on depth of soil. An abundance of perennial and annual wildflowers and grasses typical of the valley grassland community fill the open areas. Shrubs occur in drainages and under the forest canopy. Besides oaks, widespread species include California Buckeye, California Walnut, California Bay, Toyon, ceanothus species, California Flannel Bush, pines, Pacific Madrone, and manzanitas. The habitat has hot, dry summers and few or no freezing temperatures in the winter.

Central Valley Grasslands   5–30 inches precipitation/year

Hemmed in by the Coast Ranges and the Sierra Nevada, the Central Valley (aka California Dry Steppe)—a flat alluvial plain encompassing 19,200 acres—varies from sea level to an elevation of 500 feet in the lower foothills. It is laced with rivers, fed by Sierra snowmelt, and a mosaic of wetlands, alkali flats, prairies, savannas, and riparian forests. The Sacramento River joins the San Joaquin River to form an expansive delta before draining into San Francisco Bay. Historically, large expanses of seasonal flood plains and marshlands covered the valleys, triggering immense blooms of annual wildflowers; in the spring, poppies, lupines, and many other flowers and wetland plants covered the broad, rolling plains. In the summer, perennial bunchgrasses dominated. Today, vast croplands, ranches, and invasive grasses have severely altered the ecology. The wet winters and hot, dry summers are typical of the inland Mediterranean climate pattern.

Mixed-Evergreen Forest   20–60 inches precipitation/year

This community is part of the North Coastal Forest plant complex, which also includes the North Coastal Conifer Forest, Redwood Forest, and Douglas-fir Forest. Mixed-evergreen forests occur on the drier margins of the region, from the Northern Coastal mountains southward through the Central Coastal mountains, from sea level to 1,600 feet in elevation. Temperatures range from the low 20s to 90s °F. Oaks, pines, maples, Pacific Madrone, California Bay, and other canopy trees cast full to partial shade with sunny openings. This forest supports four levels of structure: Tall conifers form the canopy and broadleaf evergreens the subcanopy. Smaller trees and shrubs like Cream Bush, ceanothus, manzanitas, and California Coffeeberry populate the understory, while perennial and annual forbs and grasses, including Coyote Mint, columbines, Checker Bloom, and milkweeds, thrive at ground level. Many popular shade-tolerant landscape plants come from this community.

With so many temperature, soil, exposure, and moisture variables throughout their range, many California native plants have developed distinct varieties adapted to specific habitat niches. For nearly 100 years, horticulturalists have searched the hills, canyons, mountains, and islands for varieties with outstanding ornamental qualities: flower size, color, shape, and garden adaptability. Today, many pollinator-friendly native cultivars and hybrids are propagated for the landscape trade. Carefully choose these selections to match your garden design and sun, shade, moisture, and temperature requirements. For the greatest success and benefits to local pollinator populations, base your garden on plants that occur naturally where you live.

Before You Plant: Create a Master Plan

All too often, gardeners see a pretty plant in a nursery and make a spur-of-the-moment purchase, then plant it in a spot that gives it little chance to survive, much less thrive. The goal here is to plan ahead to create a verdant, low-maintenance garden oasis with maximum pollinator benefit and prolonged seasonal beauty while minimizing expenses from plant loss, replacement, and water usage.

Analyze Your Yard The first thing a professional landscaper would do for you is draw a plot of your yard to scale (e.g., 1 inch equals 5 or 10 feet), so that's the best way for homeowners to start as well. Nothing fancy—just sketch in existing plants, walkways, walls, and fences. Then get creative. First, consider where you want individual specimen and accent plants; then fill in more-extensive border, entry, patio, and window-view gardens; and, if you have room, include landscape ovals and islands and mass plantings. Decide where you need low-growing foreground and border flowers; medium-size midgarden plants; and taller background shrubs and trees. Noting the mature sizes in the plant profiles, leave room for the plants to fill out.

Observe Sun Exposure Along with water, the amount of sun a plant receives is perhaps the most critical factor for its survival. Plants that are native to oak woodlands, characterized by a developed understory of shade-tolerant plants, and mixed-conifer forests in the mountain ranges, can thrive in partial shade. Most vegetation in the coastal scrub and valley grasslands receives full, direct sun, broken only by filtered shade from nearby shrubs. Most native plants that thrive in the metropolitan areas require full sun to dappled shade. In the plant profiles, **Full Sun** means exposure to direct sun for 6 or more hours a day. **Partial Shade** means some full sun but with filtered shade for 4–5 hours a day, especially in the blazing afternoons. Sun-adapted plants compromised by too much shade respond with reduced blooming and leggy growth—or they die.

Now look at the shadow footprint of your house, walls, trees, and other shade-producing structures. From the shady north side of your house to the sunny southwest side, each nook and cranny creates a microhabitat guaranteed to affect how well a plant performs. Besides limiting sun exposure, a shady exposure can reduce the ground temperature in the root zone, especially in the winter, of a perennial well below the area's average low. Conversely, the reflected summer heat from a masonry wall can easily raise a plant's sustained heat load by 10°F or more.

Soil: Minerals, Nutrients & Air

A colorful California wildflower mix

Plants need about 16 essential elements to grow, flower, and produce seeds. Carbon, oxygen, and hydrogen, which produce the carbohydrates required for plant growth, come from air and water. Nitrogen (N), phosphorus (P), and potassium (K), the three main nutrients in chemical fertilizers, come from minerals and microorganisms in the soil.

Phosphorus is necessary for plant growth, photosynthesis, and sugar production. Deficiencies in nitrogen, phosphorus, or iron cause chlorosis (leaves with yellowish areas between the green veins). Zinc deficiency causes malformed and damaged leaves. The ability of roots to absorb these major and secondary compounds, and other micronutrients, depends on the pH (acidity or alkalinity) of the soil.

The mineral components of Northern California soils tend to be coarse to loamy and well draining, derived from granites, sandstones, shales, basalts, and alluvial fill. The pH varies between 7 (neutral) and 7.9 (slightly alkaline). Soils derived from decomposed granite, especially in foothills areas below granite mountains, tend to be slightly acidic. Use a pH soil-test kit, available from garden centers, if you have reason to think a serious imbalance may exist.

Serpentine soils are formed by intense heat at tectonic induction zones. These highly mineralized soils contain asbestos, copper, mercury, magnesium, and chromium but are low in calcium (limestone). Only a few plants, including 20% of California's endemic species, have adapted to survive in this soil type. Expanses of serpentine soils occur in the northern half of the state but are uncommon in the southern regions.

Native plants are perfectly adapted to thrive in a variety of native soil textures and pH, so fertilizers and soil amendments are not needed. A little compost worked into the soil surface and a thin layer of organic mulch around the plant will help retain soil moisture in hot exposures. As it matures, its own leaf litter will provide the perfect mulch.

Exotic plants and most garden vegetables adapted to soils that have a pH range of 6–7 may struggle to absorb the minerals and nutrients they need from native soils, especially phosphorus, iron, and zinc. Avoid interplanting natives with exotics that require fertilizers, more-acidic soils (in the pH range above), and lots of water.

PRECIOUS WATER, POOR SOILS

Productive semiarid garden soils contain about 50% air and 50% minerals (sand, silt, and clay). Organics in the surface layer—composted plant material, microorganisms, fungi, and bacteria—compose only about 1% of the total. The soil gaps provide oxygen necessary for the roots to respire. The spaces fill with water and the roots absorb nutrients and minerals; then the water drains and the roots breathe again.

A drought-tolerant garden

Most Northern California natives, except for some Central Valley plants, require well-draining soils and struggle in heavy clay soils, which retain water and smother roots. A simple drainage test will determine how fast your soil drains. First, dig a hole about 1 foot deep and fill it with water. Let it drain and immediately fill it again. After 15 minutes, measure how many inches of water have soaked in, and multiply by 4 to get the rate per hour. Less than 1 inch per hour means the soil is poor draining, 1–6 inches per hour is well draining, and more than 6 inches per hour is fast-draining. For gardens with clay soils and poor drainage, look for plants adapted to these soils.

The growth and bloom cycles of most native plant communities in Northern California are adapted to a Mediterranean climate pattern, consisting of winter rains and cool summers (coastal) or hot, dry summers (inland). Scrubland vegetation endures six months of summer drought by going dormant. Overwatering during dormancy is detrimental, or deadly. Vegetation along the immediate coast receives moisture from summer fog, so it is more tolerant of summer water. The western slopes of the Northern Coastal ranges have cool summers and receive enough precipitation to sustain dense coniferous forests. Choose plants adapted to your natural weather patterns for the most successful native plant gardens and landscapes.

Too little water limits blooming and growth and makes plants look rangy and unappealing in a garden setting. Too much water, especially during summer dormancy for scrubland plants, can cause root rot. After a shrub becomes established in one to two years (doubling in size), regular summer irrigation is not advised, as it kills or shortens the lives of summer-dormant plants. Soil amendments and garden soils rich in humus and organics can smother roots adapted to the high oxygen content of coarse soils. Fortunately, native plants are adaptable, so establishing a good water balance and maintaining a verdant garden aren't too difficult to manage.

One heavy storm can send hundreds of gallons of water cascading off the average roof. If you don't catch the overflow in cisterns for future watering needs, it soaks into the ground and builds up a soil moisture bank. Most urban yards are sloped away from houses so that water slowly percolates through the soil downslope, creating a simulated riparian effect. You can also incorporate a sculpted landscaped drainage into your master design so that water is not lost to runoff into the street. Depending on your base soil type, captured roof runoff could easily supply enough moisture to sustain a large tree, several shrubs, or an oval garden packed with wildflowers.

Gardening from the Ground Up

All too often, developers and their landscape architects create cookie-cutter subdivisions lined with identical yards planted with one tree and one or two shrubs—a dead zone for pollinators. With a little planning, a pollinator garden can transform a yard with an uninspired landscape, or one with high-maintenance, thirsty turf grass, into an organic, three-dimensional landscape.

A living landscape starts from the ground up—or, more precisely, with the fungus, bacteria, and other microbes several inches below the surface. Bees dig nest burrows in bare ground, beetle and moth larvae pupate just below the surface, worms and bugs decompose organic matter in the upper soil layers, butterfly and moth larvae pupate in the leaf litter, and ground-foraging birds scratch for tidbits in the soil and leaves.

Weed or Wildflower?

Coastal wildflowers in Northern California

It depends on your perspective. Many municipalities and homeowners' associations wage vicious battles against native wildflowers that grow unattended in pampered yards and medians. "Weeds!" they declare and arm themselves with herbicides. Yet to pollinators, these "volunteer" wildflowers are both rich sources of pollen and nectar and larval host plants. To a bee, the sterile petunias, pansies, hybrids, and cultivars with no pollen or nectar are worthless weeds.

California gardens are not as overrun with unwanted intruders as gardens in wetter climates, but some weed control is inevitably needed. Manual removal is usually the most efficient method, and it's far preferable to spraying a broad-spectrum herbicide with glyphosate (Roundup). Court cases with multimillion-dollar settlements, along with the World Health Organization, have ruled glyphosate a carcinogen, and many counties and municipalities in the state have banned its use on public property. A well-balanced garden with natural ground cover and healthy soil microorganisms creates its own weed control. But until a garden is established, minor weed removal may be needed with as little soil disturbance as possible.

Mulching is one of the most important ways to manage weeds and sustain a healthy, living soil. The two general types of mulch, organic and inorganic, both have a place in pollinator gardens. A modest layer (1–2 inches) of shredded bark or leaves around plants will keep the root zone cooler, slow evaporation from the soil, decrease water usage, add nutrients, and inhibit weed growth. But don't pack mulch around the base of the plant. Leave half of the root ball uncovered for the roots to breathe. The best mulch is the plant's natural leaf litter, which accumulates as the plant matures. A light layer of mulch also stabilizes open sandy areas without inhibiting ground-nesting bees and larvae. A thin, rocky mulch around a plant also has advantages. Rocks don't soak up water or seal off air from the surface roots, and they may even provide enough condensation to improve soil moisture. Also, a border of larger stones creates a microhabitat for insects that attracts ground-foraging birds.

One last consideration with your master plan is how formal you want your pollinator garden and yard landscape—neat and tidy, or more toward the wildscape look? Do you want a garden worthy of a magazine cover and a yard with trimmed shrubs and confined borders, or a naturalized habitat with a pile of limbs and leaves in the corner and a "forest" of 5-foot-tall sunflowers against the back wall? Whether you have room only for a few container plants on your balcony, a small landscape island or walkway border, or a full-scale garden design for your yard, the butterflies, bees, and birds will benefit—and you will help repair the habitat lost to our housing developments.

ABCs for a Pollinator Habitat Garden

The Xerces Society, the National Wildlife Federation, and other national and state agencies and organizations have certification programs for creating backyard wildlife habitats. They vary in particulars, but all center around certain basics: supply year-round sources of food, water, shelter, and nesting sites; plant at least 50% native plants; use no herbicides or pesticides; and avoid nursery plants treated with systemic neonicotinoids, which produce pollen and nectar poisonous to bees.

Gardens that cater specifically to pollinators have a few additional design requirements.

Water The first key element in your backyard oasis is a dependable source of water. Birds are attracted to the traditional birdbath, or you can get fancier with a solar-powered fountain, such as one with water cascading through different-size bowls. Bees like still, shallow water—a pan with pebbles on a drip emitter works great. Butterflies need moist soil, so an emitter on the ground, a garden with a drip-system mini spray, or birdbath overflow is all they need. Be sure to scrub birdbaths, bowls, and basins weekly to remove algae, fungi, and bird droppings, which could spread diseases.

Food Insect pollinators need energy-rich nectar and protein-rich pollen from the time they first emerge in the early spring, while foraging and nesting through the summer, and in the fall until they migrate or overwinter. Diversity is the rule in selecting plants, both to maintain a three-season-to-year-round bloom and to present a variety of sizes and shapes to attract a diversity of butterflies, bees, other insect pollinators, and hummingbirds. A sugar-water feeder for hummingbirds and seed feeders for birds will help supplement the natural food and seed sources. Bird droppings can transmit salmonella and other diseases, so be sure to clean feeders regularly. Thoroughly scrub sugar-water feeders, which will develop fungus in hot weather, each time you refill.

Shelter All animals need a refuge from wind, rain, midday heat, and protection from predators. Butterflies need a sunny place to bask and warm themselves in the morning, and birds need shady day perches to rest while foraging, along with leafy, protected night perches. A mix of perennial wildflowers, shrubs, a small tree, and several clumps of bunchgrasses will provide the necessary shelter.

Nest Sites A diverse population of pollinators cannot be sustained without successful nesting. For butterflies and moths, this means larval host plants. Each species lays its eggs only on the specific native plants that will nourish its caterpillars. Pretty exotic plants may supply lots of nectar and pollen, but only native plants will host the caterpillars. Most native bees are solitary and lay their eggs, along with a pollen ball for their larvae to eat, in a ground burrow they excavate or a cavity they find or drill in stems or limbs. Burrowing bees need bare ground free of thick mulch or other dense covering. Bee hotels, with holes and tubes in a variety of sizes, are popular for hole-nesting bees. Bunchgrasses harbor overwintering bees and moth larvae.

Selecting Plants

Poppies and other wildflowers

Diversity is key. Gardens with a variety of flower sizes and shapes attract the most kinds and numbers of pollinators. A well-balanced garden contains a mix of annual and long-blooming perennial flowers, along with a selection of shrubs that bloom winter–spring and summer–fall. Leafy shrubs and a small-to-medium-size tree will provide shelter from sun and wind and nesting sites for birds and bees. Also include at least two species of bunchgrass for moth larvae and overwintering bees.

You can usually look at a plant and tell what pollinates it. Some plants use a generalist strategy, which offers a rich nectar-pollen buffet to all comers. These are garden favorites because of the large numbers and kinds of pollinators they attract. Members of the aster, rose, buckwheat, and mallow families include generalist plants that attract a variety of insects.

Conversely, many plants conserve resources by catering to a select few pollinators. No garden is complete without a selection of specialty flowers that add rich colors and attract iconic pollinators. Salvias, manzanitas, penstemons, and legumes all attract specific pollinators. The special characteristics that adapt a flower to a particular class of pollinators are called **syndromes**. Syndromes are only general rules of thumb since insects will go wherever food is accessible.

PLANTING USING PLANT SYNDROMES

Bee Syndrome Flowers are shades of yellow and blue, with nectar guide lines; tubular with an inflated shape to fit bees of particular sizes; or open and bowl shaped for all bees. Petals form a landing pad; nectar glands secrete abundant nectar, with stamens producing rich pollen; flowers are faintly scented. Many members of the aster, verbena, and legume families are attractive to bees.

Butterfly Syndrome Flowers are bright reds and purples, with nectar guide lines; are tubular shaped, with a narrow throat; have petals that form a landing pad; produce more nectar than pollen (as butterflies don't gather pollen); and are faintly scented. Aside from plants rich in nectar, butterflies need host plants for their caterpillars. Almost every native plant hosts some types of caterpillars, but milkweeds are necessary for Monarchs and Queens, and they provide abundant nectar for many insects.

Moth Syndrome Flowers are white or light colored and visible in moonlight; are large and showy or small but conspicuously clustered; have a narrow, tubular throat and nocturnal or crepuscular bloom times; are strongly scented; and last one day. Various evening primroses and four o'clocks are ideal for nocturnal gardens.

Beetle Syndrome Flowers are greenish colored and dish shaped, produce abundant pollen and nectar, and are strongly scented. Beetles, some of nature's most colorful and diverse pollinators, have been pollinating flowers for 150 million years, and they feast on the pollen, petals, and developing seeds of almost any flower.

Hummingbird Syndrome Flowers are bright red to orange and tubular shaped to fit a bird's bill; they have no landing pad, guide lines, or scent, and they produce abundant nectar. Penstemons, honeysuckles, and salvias add brilliant color and attract hummingbirds, but these birds will sip from almost any flower. Maintain a sugar-water feeder (¼ cup sugar to 1 cup water) as a dependable source of food.

The Basics of Plant Anatomy

PARTS OF A FLOWER

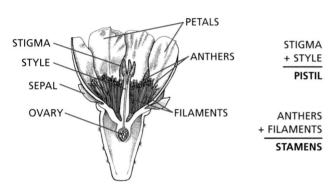

Flower anatomy has diverged radically among plant species to attract a diversity of pollinators with the twin rewards of protein-rich pollen and energy-rich nectar. From thorny cacti to flamboyant lupines, sunflowers, and penstemons, the various parts of a plant are basically the same. Yet plants have modified and perfected every anatomical feature to not only attract pollinators but also survive in the most hostile of environments.

Flowers serve one obvious purpose: to produce seeds for the continued survival of the plant. Many trees, grasses, and weedy plants eschew dependence on animal pollinators and produce nondescript flowers that scatter copious amounts of pollen to the winds. The windborne misery of hay fever victims creates a booming industry for allergy doctors and medication. Conversely, the beauty of a colorful flower inspires poetry, romance, and a wonder for the majesty of nature.

FLOWERS

The taxonomy of a flower defines the plant's species, groups it in a genus of similar plants, and assigns it to a family with broadly related features. The flower itself is a collection of modified leaves. Leaflike bracts grow on the stem beneath the flower. They are typically green, but some flowers, like paintbrushes, have bracts that are showier than the petals. **Sepals** surround and protect the bud and clasp the bottom of the flower. **Petals** are usually the showy feature and are colored and marked to attract specific pollinators. They may spread open widely or be united to form a narrow tube that opens with lobes. **Stamens,** the male feature, are thin filaments topped with pollen-covered **anthers**. The **pistil,** the female feature, consists of a tubular style, containing the ovaries, topped with a **stigma** with lobes that receive the pollen. The shape of the stamen and stigma are often highly specialized to fit certain pollinators.

FLOWER CLUSTERS

To increase pollination efficiency, flowers make gathering pollen and nectar as efficient as possible for the pollinator. Flying from flower to flower takes considerable energy, so plants with single flowers on a stem, especially annuals, are often synchronized to bloom all at the same time. Flower clusters offer dozens of small flowers together so pollinators don't have to waste energy searching. Round or flat clusters provide a compact source of nectar and pollen, while spikes of flowers usually start blooming at the bottom so flowers bloom over an extended time. Lupine and milkvetch flowers often have white banner petals that turn red when pollinated so bees won't waste energy on flowers with no more nectar. Penstemon flowers are often on one side of the spike so hummingbirds and bumblebees can simply move upward and not have to circle the stem. Members of the aster family have composite flower heads: showy, petal-like ray flowers surround a compact disk with dozens of small, tubular disk-shaped florets that produce pollen and nectar for a wide variety of pollinators.

Round to flat cluster

Spike

Composite

LEAVES

The shape, size, and color of leaves, the food factories of a plant, can offer an extra ornamental dimension to a landscape. The size of a leaf can vary from a fraction of an inch (Blue Palo Verde) to several feet long (fern and palm fronds). The shape can range from a simple oval or a deeply dissected or lobed blade to a compound leaf with dozens of tiny leaflets. To reduce water loss by transpiration, leaves and leaflets in deserts tend to be small, often with waxy or densely woolly surfaces, and may be deciduous in summer. Sun-loving plants die in the shade because sun- and shade-adapted plants produce carbohydrates using different photosynthetic pathways.

Leaves, as well as flowers, are an important feature in identifying a plant. Some flowers have a dense rosette of basal leaves, especially biennials that germinate the first year and overwinter as a rosette, then bloom the second year. Notice if the leaves grow opposite or alternate each other, or in whorls around the stem. Does the leaf clasp the stem or have a short stalk (petiole)? Are the blades simple or compound? Are the margins (edges) wavy, lobed, or smooth? Are the surfaces hairy, rough, or smooth? Leaf features all help a plant adapt to its environment.

Urban Wildlife

With the continuing loss of wildlife habitat to urban sprawl, a number of small mammals take refuge in parks, open-space preserves, greenbelts, and even vacant lots. Coyotes, foxes, feral and domestic cats, rabbits, raccoons, skunks, and other small mammals may visit pollinator gardens and backyard wildscapes from time to time. Some of these visitors, like deer and rabbits, feast on tender garden plants and may become nuisances and need to be fenced out—or delectable plants may need to be caged in. The species profiles indicate which plants are deer and rabbit resistant.

Any garden, especially one designed to be insect friendly, will attract its share of creepy-crawly visitors. You might expect to see ants, spiders, snakes, scorpions, and centipedes. Black widow spiders, with their shiny black bodies with red ventral markings, are one critter to look out for. They favor dark corners in toolsheds, woodpiles, and even underneath patio chairs and tables. Unlike orb spiders, they build chaotic, tangled webs. Bites cause varying amounts of pain and discomfort, but over-the-counter pain medication usually suffices; see a doctor if symptoms persist or become serious. Simple precautions like wearing gardening gloves when cleaning up or working in your garden usually provide ample protection. Most of these critters are delectable tidbits for ground-foraging birds and seldom become a problem.

Embracing Our Biological Heritage

Plants and pollinators are a part of our great natural heritage. Why can't our botanical neighborhoods represent the natural plant diversity that existed before our houses were built? Our children could grow up familiar with the same plants that provided food and fiber for the Indigenous peoples who have lived in California for thousands of years. The plants that first sank their roots into California soil during the last ice age can help us understand that our psyches and society are equally rooted to the earth. As our pollinator gardens flower and fruit, we will be rewarded by the sight of butterflies dancing from flower to flower and by the melodies of birds singing in our trees.

Native Plant Conservation

Because native plant populations are critical components of the ecosystem, you shouldn't collect native plants or seeds form the wild. This can harm existing plants, threaten local plant populations, and adversely affect pollinators and other wildlife that rely on them for food. What's more, collecting native plants from the wild may be illegal. Instead, always purchase or acquire native plants from the many reputable growers and nurseries. (For recommendations, see page 271 or check www.calscape.org/nurseries.php.)

Meet the Pollinators

Fossil records of beetles and flowers indicate that the pollination saga began about 150 million years ago. Since then, bees, butterflies, moths, flies, and wasps have joined the diverse cast, but the flowers themselves have always retained ultimate control of the show. The floral masters of manipulation have devised ways beyond the limits of human imagination to direct pollinator behavior. Using rewards (energy-rich nectar and protein-rich pollen), deception, false advertising, bait and switch, entrapment, and even lethal measures, flowers engineer insects to transport their pollen in the most energy-efficient ways. This eons-old drama continues today on every flower in your pollinator garden.

BEES

California, with its diversity of blooming plants, is a paradise for bees. Of the more than 4,000 species that live in North America, at least 1,600 call our state home. Native bees are up to 200 times more efficient at pollination than the domestic honeybee. These rock stars of the pollinator world are the only animals that deliberately collect pollen. Adult bees feed on nectar, and, with special hairs designed to hold pollen grains, the females collect pollen to store in their brood chambers for larvae to eat. Most bees are generalist feeders, but some prefer a specific family, genus, or even a single species of flowering plants. Though the bumblebee clan is social, 90% of bees are solitary, with each female creating her own set of brood chambers. She digs a burrow in bare ground, tunnels into a plant stem, or uses a preexisting cavity. In a garden setting, easily constructed "bee hotels," drilled with holes in different sizes, often fill up quickly.

At the end of her life—only about six weeks as an adult—the female seals off the last chamber and dies. The larvae develop over the winter and emerge in the spring, just in time for the early-blooming flowers. By some unknown clues, specialty feeders synchronize their emergence with the bloom of their preferred species. Some may extend their dormancy several years if droughts suppress blooming.

Bees in California vary in size from smaller than a grain of rice to robust, 1-inch-long bumblebees. Large bees can forage over distances of more than a mile, medium-size bees range over 400–500 yards, small bees venture 200 yards, and tiny bees can be confined to 200 feet. Ideally, the population of bees in your garden will be able to find the food and nesting sites in your and your neighbors' backyard gardens to complete their entire life cycle.

1. Valley Carpenter Bee (*Xylocopa sonorina*) **2.** Western Honeybee (*Apis mellifera*) **3.** Cactus Bee (*Lithurgopsis* spp.)
4. Metallic Green Bee (*Agapostemon melliventris*) **5.** Megachile Bee (*Megachile* spp.) **6.** Hunt's Bumblebee (*Bombus huntii*)

BUTTERFLIES

Central and Northern California harbor one of the most diverse butterfly populations in North America. Of the approximately 800 species of butterflies in North America, more than 270 (by some counts) occur in California. In the Bay Area alone, 144 species have been recorded, 3 of those on the federal endangered species list, mainly due to habitat loss and pesticide use.

The western migration of the Monarch Butterfly brings hundreds of thousands of this species from west of the Rockies to overwinter in protected groves on the Central Coast. In the 1980s, 4.5 million Monarchs migrated to about five coastal sites. By 2010, the numbers had dropped to 200,000, then to 30,000 in 2018. In 2020, the totals plummeted drastically to 2,000, rebounding somewhat in 2021. The main culprit: habitat loss.

With brilliant colors and intricate patterns, these charismatic insects are one of the star attractions in a pollinator garden. Ironically, in the scheme of efficient pollination, butterflies fall near the bottom of the list. With long legs that often hold them above the flower's pollen-bearing anthers, a long tongue to probe deep into the flower, and no body hair designed to collect pollen, butterflies pollinate by accident, not design. Even so, they are critically important to the health and stability of the ecosystem's complex food chain.

During their adult life span of 1–2 weeks, females lay hundreds of eggs on specific host plants. The eggs hatch into caterpillars, which relentlessly devour plant foliage. They increase their body mass by up to 10,000 times before entering metamorphosis. These juicy tidbits of protein feed the world of the wild. The majority (95%) of all songbirds depend on caterpillar protein to nourish their hatchlings.

In the winter or in times of drought, butterflies go into **diapause,** a period of suspended growth similar to hibernation. Diapause can occur in any life stage: egg, larva, chrysalis, or adult. A butterfly may be several years old by the time it becomes an adult. During winter diapause, caterpillars (of both butterflies and moths) nest in fallen leaves, bunchgrass stubble, or underground; chrysalides hang on protected twigs; and adults hide in woodpiles, cracks, or under loose bark. So when you tidy up your garden in the winter, be sure to reserve a place for overwintering butterflies and moths.

Darting from flower to flower or dancing in the sunlight overhead, butterflies delight all ages. My preschool daughter called them "flutterbys," which I think best describes these amazing creatures.

1. Great Bluish Green Hairstreak (*Atlides halesus*) **2.** Gulf Fritillary (*Agraulis vanillae*) **3.** Monarch (*Danaus plexippus*)
4. Two-Tailed Swallowtail (*Papilio multicaudata*) **5.** Pipevine Swallowtail (*Battus philenor*) **6.** Painted Lady (*Vanessa cardui*)

MOTHS

As night falls, nature's night shift takes over. In a pollinator garden, that means moths, one of the most numerous and efficient classes of pollinators. There are about 12,000 moth species in the US and about 900 in California, outnumbering butterfly species 13 to 1. Male moths have feathery, comblike antennae, while females' are smooth and pointed; in contrast, butterflies have smooth antennae with a swollen, clublike tip. Moths vary in size from ¼ inch to hummingbird-size sphinxes and hawk moths. They can be diurnal (Police Car Moths), but most are crepuscular (sphinxes and hawk moths) or nocturnal.

Moths have the same metamorphic life cycle and host plant requirements as butterflies, but more are plant specialists. Many plants have long floral tubes pollinated only by long-tongued moths, or they emit puffs of sweet aroma into the night to attract moths from far distances. Sacred Datura produces a sugar-rich nectar laced with addictive hallucinogens to keep sphinx moths coming back night after night. As another example, each species of yucca depends on a single species of moth for pollination. The moth gathers pollen from one yucca and then deposits it in the specially shaped stigma of a nearby yucca, then lays her eggs in the ovary so the larvae can eat the developing seeds. The larvae pupate in the ground and don't emerge until the yucca flowers again, which can take years.

The Oakworm, or Oak Moth larva (*Phryganidia californica*), is one of dozens of moth larvae that feed on oak leaves in California. Periodically, it defoliates oaks throughout a wide area, but healthy oaks quickly rebound with new leaves. The use of insecticides is not recommended by the Integrated Pest Management Program of the University of California Agriculture and Natural Resources. Instead of spraying, let nature's balance take its course.

Moths are a vital part of the ecosystem food chain. Most songbirds (95%) feed their nestlings moth caterpillars found on tree and shrub leaves, and many ground-foraging birds feast on the nearly 50% of moths that pupate in leaf litter, bunchgrass thatch, and shallow soil. So be sure to include some wild space in your habitat, and a selection of night-blooming wildflowers in your garden, such as Sacred Datura in the nightshade family (Solanaceae), and members of the evening primrose (Onagraceae) and four o'clock (Nyctaginaceae) families.

1. White-Lined Sphinx Moth (*Hyles lineata*) **2.** Snowberry Clearwing Moth (*Hemaris diffinis*) **3.** Columbia Silk Moth (*Hyalophora columbia*) **4.** Rustic Sphinx Moth (*Manduca rustica*) **5.** Army Cutworm Moth (*Euxoa auxiliaris*) **6.** Tiger Moth (*Pyrrharctia isabella*)

FLIES

This diverse order, with 125,000 species worldwide, includes many that are important pollinators. As pollinators, flies are second in importance to bees. Flies have been recorded visiting at least 71 plant families. At higher altitudes with cold mornings and during cloudy or inclement weather, flies are active much longer during the day than bees. Flies vary in size from mere specks to an inch long. Many native flies are hairy and easily confused for bees, but flies have nubby antennae and big eyes, while bees have long antennae and smaller eyes.

Flies, especially hover flies (family Syrphidae), are an important component of a pollinator habitat. The adults feed on nectar as they pollinate, and the larvae help control insect damage to plants. As carnivorous predators, the larvae complete the food web by feeding on aphids, spiders, other insects, and detritus. Most flies have short tongues and feed on shallow, flat flowers. They are critical pollinators for many plants in the carrot/parsley (Apiaceae) and aster (Asteraceae) families; many annuals and small-flowering shade plants; and more than 100 human food plants, including cacao (chocolate), carrots, tree fruits, berries, avocados, and mangoes.

1. Bee Fly (*Hemipenthes* spp.) **2.** Grasshopper Bee Fly (*Systoechus vulgaris*) **3.** Flower Fly (*Syrphus* spp.) **4.** Red Tachinid Fly (*Adejeania vexatrix*) **5.** Beelike Tachinid Fly (*Hystricia abrupta*) **6.** Tachinid Fly (Tachinidae genera)

BEETLES

Though they are thought to be the first insects to start the complex coevolutionary relationship between insects and flowers 150 million years ago, beetles are minor players in the saga today. Yet with 30,000 species in the United States, and 340,000 and counting around the world, the impact of beetles on the plant world is immense. Though much of their activity is detrimental, such as the devastation of conifer forests by bark beetles, they play critical roles as pollinators, decomposers, and predators—for example, ladybugs eat aphids both as larvae and adults. Beetles are necessary and beneficial in a well-balanced habitat and generally welcomed inhabitants in our gardens. A number of beetle families are important pollinators, but they do so more by their clumsy rambling over flowers as they gulp nectar; munch away on pollen, petals, and flower parts; and search for sex partners. Scores of small beetles may congregate in a single cactus flower, and dozens of soldier beetles may crawl over the dense flower heads of goldenrods, while a single red-and-black flower beetle poses like the king of a flower. Beetles are some of the most bizarre and flamboyantly colored insects you'll find in nature, and they are thrilling visitors in your garden.

1. Fire-Colored Beetle (*Pyrochroa* spp.) **2.** Goldenrod Soldier Beetle (*Chauliognathus pennsylvanicus*) **3.** Longhorn Beetle (*Crossidius humeralis*) **4.** Red Longhorn Beetle (*Crossidius militaris*) **5.** Spotted Tylosis Longhorn Beetle (*Tylosis maculatus*) **6.** Soldier Beetle (*Chauliognathus* spp.)

BIRDS

According to the National Audubon Society, Americans spend more money on bird food and binoculars than on hunting and ammunition. By supplying the habitat needs of birds, your back window or patio can be an exciting place to watch birds. A yard oasis with shrubs and trees for nesting and shelter, fruit- and seed-bearing plants and a seed feeder for dependable food, and a constant water source will support year-round resident birds and attract seasonal migrants.

With a mild coastal Mediterranean climate and year-round blooming flowers, Central and Northern California host a diverse population of resident birdlife, including nine species of breeding hummingbirds. To attract resident and migrant hummingbirds, stock your garden with plants that have red, tubular flowers, such as salvias, penstemons, and Hummingbird Trumpet, supplemented with a sugar-water feeder to ensure a constant food source.

In the spring and fall each year, millions of waterfowl and songbirds migrate along the Pacific Flyway, mainly along the coast and through the Central Valley. Many songbirds and hummingbirds overwinter in Mexico, and on their way there, they make daily stops to refuel in natural habitat, refuges and sanctuaries, or wildlife-friendly backyards that provide food, water, and shelter.

How to Use This Book

The native plants in this book are organized by type, with sections for **Trees, Shrubs, Wildflowers,** and **Vines & Grasses**. Each plant profile includes key information about the plant's size and growth pattern, hardiness zone, bloom period, companion plants, and what it attracts, as well as a more detailed description of the plant.

You can either find plants that strike your fancy by paging through the profiles in the body of the book, or you can consult the information in the back. See page 258 for a list of plants that attract butterflies, page 260 for plants that attract bees, page 264 for plants that attract feeding and nesting birds, and page 265 for plants that specifically attract hummingbirds. Page 262 lists plants that are good for container gardening. Page 268 has a list of butterflies/moths with host plants for their caterpillars.

For information and inspiration, visit one of the botanical gardens listed on page 274 to see and compare mature native plants in landscape settings; then you can draw a plot of your garden and sketch in prospective plants. Turn to page 271 for a list of native plant retail suppliers in Northern California. Finally, check page 273 for a list of **Northern California Native Plant Society** chapters.

Northern California Plants at a Glance

The at-a-glance table on the next page includes each plant's hardiness zone and blooming period; indicates whether a plant attracts butterflies, bees, or birds; and lists its likely deer/rabbit resistance.

For a well-balanced garden, select plants that will provide blooms from early spring through winter. To maximize pollinator numbers and diversity, choose a mix of flowers in a variety of sizes and shapes.

Also remember that no plant is totally resistant to a hungry deer or rabbit—if necessary, enclose young, tender plants in a wire cage.

Northern California Plants at a Glance

COMMON NAME	SCIENTIFIC NAME	NORTHERN CALIFORNIA HARDINESS ZONES
TREES		
Blue Elderberry pg. 39	Sambucus nigra ssp. cerulea	6b–10b
California Bay pg. 41	Umbellularia californica	7b–10a
California Buckeye pg. 43	Aesculus californica	6b–10b
Hollyleaf Cherry pg. 45	Prunus ilicifolia ssp. ilicifolia	8b–10a
Pacific Madrone pg. 47	Arbutus menziesii	7b–9b
Pacific Wax Myrtle pg. 49	Morella californica (Myrica californica)	8a–10b
Western Redbud pg. 51	Cercis occidentalis	7a–9b
SHRUBS		
Blueblossom pg. 55	Ceanothus thyrsiflorus	8b–10b
Blue Witches pg. 57	Solanum xanti	7a–10b
Bush Anemone pg. 59	Carpenteria californica	8a–10b
Bush Monkeyflower pg. 61	Diplacus aurantiacus	8b–10b
California Buckwheat pg. 63	Eriogonum fasciculatum	7b–10b
California Coffeeberry pg. 65	Frangula californica	8a–9b
California Flannel Bush pg. 67	Fremontodendron californicum	8b–10b
California Mountain Lilac pg. 69	Ceanothus 'Concha'	8a–10b
California Wild Rose pg. 71	Rosa californica	6a–10b
'Canyon Silver' Catalina Silver-Lace, pg. 73	Constancea nevinii 'Canyon Silver'	9b–10b
Chamise pg. 75	Adenostoma fasciculatum	8a–10a

ATTRACTS BUTTERFLIES	ATTRACTS BEES	ATTRACTS BIRDS	BLOOM PERIOD	DEER RESISTANT
nectar, host	yes	fruit, shelter	March–May; fruit: September–October	no (young), yes (mature)
nectar, host	yes	shelter	March–May	yes
yes	yes	shelter	April–June	no
nectar, host	yes	fruit, shelter	March–May; fruit: August	no
yes	yes	fruit, shelter (hummingbirds)	January–May; fruit: September	yes
yes	yes	fruit, shelter	March–July	yes
yes	yes	seeds, shelter	February–April	yes
yes	yes	no	February–May	no
nectar, host	yes	fruit	February–July	yes
yes	yes	shelter	May–July	yes
nectar, host	yes	yes	March–June; fall (depending on environmental factors)	yes
nectar, host	yes	seeds	April–September	yes
nectar, host	yes	fruit, shelter	June–August	yes
nectar, host	yes	shelter	March–July	yes
nectar, host	yes	shelter	March–May	yes
nectar, host	yes	shelter	April–August	yes
nectar, host	yes	seeds	April–September	yes
nectar, host	yes	shelter	June–August	yes

	COMMON NAME	SCIENTIFIC NAME	NORTHERN CALIFORNIA HARDINESS ZONES
	Chaparral Currant pg. 77	*Ribes malvaceum*	7a–10b
	Chaparral Mallow pg. 79	*Malacothamnus fasciculatus*	8b–10b
	Chokecherry pg. 81	*Prunus virginiana*	5a–10b
	Cleveland Sage pg. 83	*Salvia clevelandii*	8a–10b
	Common Snowberry pg. 85	*Symphoricarpos albus var. laevigatus*	5a–9b
	Coyote Brush pg. 87	*Baccharis pilularis ssp. pilularis*	7b–10b
	Cream Bush pg. 89	*Holodiscus discolor*	5b–10a
	Dr. Hurd Manzanita pg. 91	*Arctostaphylos manzanita* 'Dr. Hurd'	8a–10b
	Fragrant Sumac pg. 93	*Rhus aromatica*	5b–10b
	Fuchsia-Flowered Gooseberry pg. 95	*Ribes speciosum*	8a–10b
	Giant Coreopsis pg. 97	*Coreopsis gigantea* (*Leptosyne gigantea*)	9b–10a
	Golden Currant pg. 99	*Ribes aureum*	5a–10b
	Golden Yarrow pg. 101	*Eriophyllum confertiflorum*	7b–11a
	Heartleaf Keckiella pg. 103	*Keckiella cordifolia*	6b–10a
	Howard McMinn Manzanita pg. 105	*Arctostaphylos densiflora* 'Howard McMinn'	7a–10b
	Hummingbird Trumpet pg. 107	*Epilobium canum*	7a–10b
	Island Bush Poppy pg. 109	*Dendromecon harfordii*	7b–10a
	Island Snapdragon pg. 111	*Gambelia speciosa*	9a–10b
	Lilac Verbena pg. 113	*Verbena lilacina*	7a–10b
	Malva Rosa pg. 115	*Malva assurgentiflora*	9a–10b
	Naked Buckwheat pg. 117	*Eriogonum nudum*	5b–10b

ATTRACTS BUTTERFLIES	ATTRACTS BEES	ATTRACTS BIRDS	BLOOM PERIOD	DEER RESISTANT
yes	yes	fruit (hummingbirds)	December–April	yes
nectar, host	yes	seeds	April–July	yes
yes	yes	fruit, shelter	May–June; fruit: summer	yes
nectar, host	yes	seeds	April–July	yes
nectar, host	yes	fruit, shelter	May–July; fruit: fall–winter	yes
yes	yes	shelter	October–January	yes
nectar, host	yes	shelter	May–August	yes
yes	yes	fruit, shelter	January–March	yes
nectar, host	yes	seeds, shelter	March–May; fruit: July–October	yes
nectar, host	yes	fruit (hummingbirds)	January–May	yes
nectar, host	yes	no	January–May	no (young), yes (mature)
nectar, host	yes	fruit	April–June	yes
nectar, host	yes	no	January–August	yes
nectar, host	yes	seeds, shelter	May–July	yes
nectar, host	yes	fruit, shelter	February–April	yes
nectar, host	yes	hummingbirds	August–September	yes
nectar, host	yes	shelter	March–July	no
yes	yes	hummingbirds	February–June	yes
nectar, host	yes	no	March–October (inland), year-round (coastal)	yes
nectar, host	yes	seeds, shelter	February–July; September–October	no
yes	yes	seeds	May–August	yes

	COMMON NAME	SCIENTIFIC NAME	NORTHERN CALIFORNIA HARDINESS ZONES
	Oregon Grape pg. 119	*Berberis aquifolium* 'Golden Abundance'	6a–8b
	Our Lord's Candle pg. 121	*Hesperoyucca whipplei*	8b–10a
	Pacific Ninebark pg. 123	*Physocarpus capitatus*	5a–10b
	Pink-Flowering Currant pg. 125	*Ribes sanguineum* var. *glutinosum*	8b–10b
	Red Osier Dogwood pg. 127	*Cornus sericea*	5a–10b
	Salal pg. 129	*Gaultheria shallon*	8a–10b
	Santa Cruz Buckwheat pg. 131	*Eriogonum arborescens*	7b–10b
	Silver Bush Lupine pg. 133	*Lupinus albifrons*	8a–10a
	St. Catherine's Lace pg. 135	*Eriogonum giganteum*	8b–10b
	Toyon pg. 137	*Heteromeles arbutifolia*	7a–10b
	Twinberry Honeysuckle pg. 139	*Lonicera involucrata* var. *ledebourii*	6a–10b
	Western Azalea pg. 141	*Rhododendron occidentale*	6a–10b
	Western Mock Orange pg. 143	*Philadelphus lewisii*	5a–10b
	Western Spice Bush pg. 145	*Calycanthus occidentalis*	7a–10b
	Western Spirea pg. 147	*Spiraea douglasii*	5a–10b
	Woolly Blue Curls pg. 149	*Trichostema lanatum*	7a–10b
	Yankee Point Ceanothus pg. 151	*Ceanothus griseus* 'Yankee Point'	8a–10b

WILDFLOWERS

	COMMON NAME	SCIENTIFIC NAME	NORTHERN CALIFORNIA HARDINESS ZONES
	Baby Blue Eyes pg. 155	*Nemophila menziesii*	7b–11a
	Blue-Eyed Grass pg. 157	*Sisyrinchium bellum*	7a–10b
	Broadleaf Lupine pg. 159	*Lupinus latifolius*	5b–10b

ATTRACTS BUTTERFLIES	ATTRACTS BEES	ATTRACTS BIRDS	BLOOM PERIOD	DEER RESISTANT
host (moths)	yes	fruit, nesting	March–May	yes
yes	yes	nesting	April–May	yes
yes	yes	seeds, shelter	May–June	yes
nectar, host	yes	fruit	February–April	yes
nectar, host	yes	fruit, shelter	April–June	no
host	yes	fruit, shelter	April–May; fruit: July–September	yes
yes	yes	seeds	April–October	yes
nectar, host	yes	no	March–July	yes
nectar, host	yes	seeds, shelter	March–August	yes
nectar, host	yes	fruit, shelter	June–August; fruit: fall–winter	no (young), yes (mature)
yes	yes	fruit, shelter	April–July	yes
yes	yes	shelter	May–June	yes
yes	yes	seeds, shelter	May–June	yes
yes	yes	shelter	April–August	yes
yes	yes	shelter	July–August	yes
nectar, host	yes	hummingbirds	March–August	yes
nectar, host	yes	shelter	February–June	no
nectar, host	yes	no	February–June	no
yes	yes	no	March–May	yes
yes	yes	no	April–July	yes

COMMON NAME	SCIENTIFIC NAME	NORTHERN CALIFORNIA HARDINESS ZONES
California Bee Plant pg. 161	*Scrophularia californica*	7a–10b
California Goldenrod pg. 163	*Solidago velutina* ssp. *californica*	6a–10b
California Golden Violet pg. 165	*Viola pedunculata*	8b–11a
California Goldfields pg. 167	*Lasthenia californica*	7a–10b
California Poppy pg. 169	*Eschscholzia californica*	8a–10b
Canyon (Red) Larkspur pg. 171	*Delphinium nudicaule*	7a–11a
Checker Bloom pg. 173	*Sidalcea malviflora*	6a–10a
Chinese Houses pg. 175	*Collinsia heterophylla*	7a–10b
Coast Aster pg. 177	*Symphyotrichum chilense*	6a–10b
Coast Buckwheat pg. 179	*Eriogonum latifolium*	8a–11a
Common Madia pg. 181	*Madia elegans*	All zones
Common Sunflower pg. 183	*Helianthus annuus*	2a–11a
Common Woolly Sunflower pg. 185	*Eriophyllum lanatum*	5b–10b
Coyote Mint pg. 187	*Monardella villosa*	8b–10b
Douglas Iris pg. 189	*Iris douglasiana*	9b–10b
Farewell to Spring pg. 191	*Clarkia amoena*	7a–10b
Foothill Penstemon pg. 193	*Penstemon heterophyllus*	7b–10b
Globe Gilia pg. 195	*Gilia capitata*	All zones
Hairy Gumplant pg. 197	*Grindelia hirsutula*	8a–10b
Hooker's Evening Primrose pg. 199	*Oenothera elata*	5a–10b
Hummingbird Sage pg. 201	*Salvia spathacea*	7a–10b

ATTRACTS BUTTERFLIES	ATTRACTS BEES	ATTRACTS BIRDS	BLOOM PERIOD	DEER RESISTANT
yes	yes	seeds (hummingbirds)	April–July	yes
nectar, host	yes	no	July–October	yes
yes	yes	no	February–April	yes
yes	yes	no	March–May	yes
nectar, host	yes	seeds	February–June	yes
no	yes	hummingbirds	March–July	yes
nectar, host	yes	hummingbirds	May–August	yes
yes	yes	no	February–April	yes
nectar, host	yes	seeds	June–October	yes
yes	yes	no	July–September	yes
yes	yes	seeds	June–November	yes
nectar, host	yes	seeds	June–August	yes
yes	yes	no	May–August	yes
nectar, host	yes	hummingbirds	June–August	yes
no	yes	no	February–June	yes
yes	yes	no	June–August	yes
yes	yes	hummingbirds	May–July	yes
nectar, host	yes	no	February–July	yes
yes	yes	seeds	June–September	yes
nectar, host	yes	hummingbirds	June–September	no
nectar, host	yes	hummingbirds	March–May	yes

COMMON NAME	SCIENTIFIC NAME	NORTHERN CALIFORNIA HARDINESS ZONES
Indian Pink pg. 203	*Silene laciniata* ssp. *californica*	8b–10b
Leopard Lily pg. 205	*Lilium pardalinum*	5b–10b
Meadowfoam pg. 207	*Limnanthes douglasii*	5a–10b
Narrowleaf Milkweed pg. 209	*Asclepias fascicularis*	7a–10b
Redwood Sorrel pg. 211	*Oxalis oregana*	7b–9b
Sacred Datura pg. 213	*Datura wrightii*	6a–11a
Scarlet Bugler Penstemon pg. 215	*Penstemon centranthifolius*	8b–10b
Seaside Daisy pg. 217	*Erigeron glaucus*	8b–10b
Self-Heal pg. 219	*Prunella vulgaris*	5a–9a
Showy Milkweed pg. 221	*Asclepias speciosa*	3a–9b
Spreading Coastal Gumplant pg. 223	*Grindelia stricta* var. *platyphylla*	9a–10b
Sulphur Buckwheat pg. 225	*Eriogonum umbellatum*	5a–10a
Tansy-Leaf Phacelia pg. 227	*Phacelia tanacetifolia*	5a–10b
Tidy Tips pg. 229	*Layia platyglossa*	All zones
Western Pearly Everlasting pg. 231	*Anaphalis margaritacea*	3a–10a
Western Red Columbine pg. 233	*Aquilegia formosa*	7a–10a
Yarrow pg. 235	*Achillea millefolium*	5b–10b
Yellow Sand-Verbena pg. 237	*Abronia latifolia*	9b–10b

VINES & GRASSES

COMMON NAME	SCIENTIFIC NAME	NORTHERN CALIFORNIA HARDINESS ZONES
Anacapa Pink Island Morning Glory, pg. 241	*Calystegia macrostegia* 'Anacapa Pink'	7b–10b
California Dutchman's Pipe pg. 243	*Aristolochia californica*	8a–10b

ATTRACTS BUTTERFLIES	ATTRACTS BEES	ATTRACTS BIRDS	BLOOM PERIOD	DEER RESISTANT
yes	yes	hummingbirds	April–July	yes
yes	no	hummingbirds	June–July	no
yes	yes	no	March–July	yes
nectar, host	yes	no	May–October	yes
yes	yes	no	February–September	yes
sphinx moths	yes	no	April–November	yes
nectar, host	yes	hummingbirds	March–July	no (young), yes (mature)
nectar, host	yes	no	April–September	yes
yes	yes	seeds	June–August	yes
nectar, host	yes	no	June–July	yes
nectar, host	yes	seeds	May–October	yes
nectar, host	yes	seeds	February–June	yes
nectar, host	yes	no	March–May	yes
yes	yes	no	February–March	no
yes	yes	no	June–September	yes
nectar, host	yes	hummingbirds	April–October	yes
nectar, host	yes	no	April–August	yes
yes	yes	no	March–October	yes
nectar, host	yes	no	February–August	yes
host	no	no	January–April	yes

Northern California Plants at a Glance (continued)

	COMMON NAME	SCIENTIFIC NAME	NORTHERN CALIFORNIA HARDINESS ZONES
	California Fescue pg. 245	*Festuca californica*	7a–11a
	California Wild Grape pg. 247	*Vitis californica*	8b–10b
	Canyon Prince Wild Rye pg. 249	*Leymus condensatus* 'Canyon Prince'	7b–10b
	Deer Grass pg. 251	*Muhlenbergia rigens*	6a–10b
	Mendocino Leafy Reed Grass pg. 253	*Calamagrostis foliosa*	8a–10b
	Pink Honeysuckle pg. 255	*Lonicera hispidula*	8a–11a
	Virgin's Bower Clematis pg. 257	*Clematis ligusticifolia*	5a–10b

Western Red Columbine

ATTRACTS BUTTERFLIES	ATTRACTS BEES	ATTRACTS BIRDS	BLOOM PERIOD	DEER RESISTANT
yes	shelter	seeds	May–June	yes
yes	yes	fruit, shelter	May–June; fruit: July–September	no
host (moths)	shelter	seeds	June–August	yes
host	shelter	no	June–September	yes
yes	shelter	no	May–November	yes
nectar, host	yes	shelter, hummingbirds	April–July; fruit: September	yes
nectar, host	yes	shelter	June–September	yes

Pacific Wax Myrtle

Trees

Hollyleaf Cherry

California Bay

Blue Elderberry

Trees are among the most important—and beautiful—components of a yard landscape and pollinator habitat. From coastal scrub through chaparral brushlands, oak woodlands, and conifer forests, trees have adapted to become keystone members of the ecosystem. Several small trees will fit into a home-scale landscape and provide food and shelter for birds and insect pollinators, host plants for butterflies and moths, and resting and nesting sites. The trees profiled here have showy flowers and foliage, and abundant fruit or seeds.

Western Redbud

Blue Elderberry

Scientific Name *Sambucus nigra* ssp. *cerulea*

Family Moschatel (Adoxaceae)

Plant Characteristics Fast-growing, deciduous, leafy, 10-foot-tall shrub to 20-foot tree, often with multiple trunks; leaves are compound, with 5–9 lance-shaped leaflets; large clusters of creamy flowers are followed by blue-black berries. Young foliage is deer palatable, while mature foliage is deer resistant.

USDA Hardiness Zones 6b–10b

Bloom Period Spring (March–May); fruit: September–October

Growing Conditions Performs best in full sun to partial shade, tolerates full shade; rich, moist, well-draining soils; water 2x/month depending on conditions.

With ornate trunks, showy flowers, and an abundance of delectable fruit, this fast-growing small tree or shrub quickly becomes the rock star of a pollinator habitat garden. Large clusters of flowers delight numerous pollinators in the spring, and the berries are an important food for many birds in the fall. Native to streamsides, valleys, and forest openings, Blue Elderberry likes periodic deep watering but is very drought tolerant once established. It can be shaped as a shrub or an ornate tree with one or multiple trunks. For a mix of color and texture, pair it with Toyon (red berries), currants, Oregon Grape, or Red Osier Dogwood, or underplant it with California Fuchsia, Lilac Verbena, or Hummingbird Sage. The ripe berries can be used for wine, jam, and pies. The more northern Red Elderberry (*S. racemosa*) has red berries that are toxic to humans, if not prepared correctly.

Attracts bees, butterflies; pollinated by native flies; provides nesting, shelter, winter food for birds; larval host for up to 23 moth species.

California Bay

Scientific Name *Umbellularia californica*

Family Laurel (Lauraceae)

Plant Characteristics Evergreen tree typically 15–45 feet tall, with erect branches and a dense crown or, in dry habitats, a leafy shrub 6 feet tall; leaves oblong, leathery, glossy, aromatic, with a volatile, camphorlike oil; flowers small, yellowish green, clustered; fruit a green drupe, purple when mature, ½ inch in diameter. Deer resistant.

USDA Hardiness Zones 7b–10a

Bloom Period Spring (March–May)

Growing Conditions Full sun (fast growing)–deep shade (slow growing); rich, moist, well-draining soils; water 3x/month once established.

Native to canyons and valleys in chaparral, oak woodlands, and redwood forests, this adaptable tree thrives in landscape conditions. With glossy, evergreen leaves and ornate flowers and fruit, this laurel is a premier addition to a medium- to large-scale bird and pollinator garden. Give it full sun in areas with 30 inches of rain per year, along with lots of patience, and you'll get a towering specimen that creates deep shade. In drier habitats with thin soils, the evergreen is happy as a small tree or shrub. Excellent as a tall screen, natural or sheared hedge, or even a container plant for a patio or poolside. The foliage is highly aromatic, with volatile oils that tend to inhibit understory growth. For added garden color, mix with compatible shrubs such as Bush Monkeyflower, ceanothus selections, California Coffeeberry, Toyon, and California Flannel Bush.

Attracts numerous insects; provides shelter, nesting for birds; larval host for up to 4 moth species.

California Buckeye

Scientific Name *Aesculus californica*

Family Soapberry (Sapindaceae)

Plant Characteristics Deciduous, multitrunked tree 10–25 feet tall and wide; leaves palmately compound, with oval leaflets; drought deciduous July–February; small, white flowers form dense, 4- to 12-inch-long clusters; seed a capsule 1–3 inches wide, brown, poisonous. Foliage palatable to deer.

USDA Hardiness Zones 6b–10b

Bloom Period Spring–summer (April–June)

Growing Conditions Full sun, partial shade; coarse, loamy, moist-to-dry, medium-draining soils; water 2x/month max once established.

Native to dry slopes and along waterways, buckeye is a dominant plant in chaparral and oak woodlands in Northern California's Mediterranean climate. New leaves emerge in the spring, followed by dense clusters of fragrant flowers that are a nectar-rich bonanza, especially for spring-migrating butterflies. By early summer, the leaves turn brown and drop, leaving a dramatic focal point of bare, twisted, spreading limbs. Along the coast, extra summer water delays leaf fall. The cultivar 'Canyon Pink' has flamboyant pink flowers. For year-round color and foliage texture, partner with low-growing manzanita and ceanothus selections, Bush Monkeyflower, and sun-loving flowers such as buckwheats, Coyote Mint, and California Goldenrod. *Note:* Buckeye nectar is poisonous to domestic honeybees, but they tend to avoid the flowers if alternatives are available.

Attracts native bees, butterflies, and other pollinators; provides shelter for birds; larval host for Pacific Azure Butterfly (Celastrina echo) and up to 11 moth species.

Hollyleaf Cherry

Scientific Name *Prunus ilicifolia* ssp. *ilicifolia*

Family Rose (Rosaceae)

Plant Characteristics Moderate- to fast-growing, evergreen tree 10–30 feet tall; leaves oval, holly-like, with spiny-toothed-to-smooth edges; creamy flowers in dense, slender clusters; fruit a dark-red drupe ⅝ inch in diameter. Palatable to deer.

USDA Hardiness Zones 8b–10a

Bloom Period Spring (March–May); fruit: summer (August)

Growing Conditions Full sun, partial shade; coarse, well-draining, fertile soils; water 1–2x/month.

Native to chaparral and foothill woodlands along the coast from San Francisco to Los Angeles, this evergreen with ornate leaves, flowers, and fruit is a four-season superstar for your habitat garden. It checks all the boxes for birds, bees, butterflies. In the spring, clusters of creamy-white flowers attract insects; in the summer, birds dine on an abundance of red berries, and butterfly and moth larvae love to munch on the glossy leaves. The rounded shape and compact, leafy canopy, with its dense shade, provide a year-round foliage accent. It's suitable as a natural or sheared specimen, background border, screen planting, or a mixed-species hedge. Complementary large-scale flowering shrubs include Toyon, Blue Elderberry, California Coffeeberry, and California Flannel Bush. Catalina Island Cherry (subspecies *lyonii*) is larger and not as cold hardy.

Attracts bees and butterflies; provides summer fruit and shelter for birds; larval host for more than 100 butterfly and moth species, including swallowtail and hairsteak butterflies and sphinx moths.

Pacific Madrone

Scientific Name *Arbutus menziesii*

Family Heath (Ericaceae)

Plant Characteristics Evergreen shrub or tree typically 15–60 feet tall and wide, with ornate, twisting branches; smooth, red bark; and bright-green leaves up to 5 inches long; small, creamy flowers are urn shaped, in large, dangling clusters; fruit red, ½ inch around, fleshy. Deer resistant.

USDA Hardiness Zones 7b–9b; has low tolerance to sustained frost.

Bloom Period Winter–spring (January–May); fruit: September

Growing Conditions Partial shade, full sun; rocky, fine-textured, rapid-draining soils; water 1x/month max in summer.

Given patience, ideal growing conditions, and a smile from the horticulture gods, this stunning tree will highlight your yard for decades. Start small with a gallon seedling placed in bright shade or under a mother plant, such as an oak. Ensure rapid-draining soil to prevent root rot, mulch the roots to protect it from summer heat, and be patient as it grows from shrubby to tree size. If you replicate the dry summers and moderate, wet winters common to its native open oak woodlands and conifer forests, your madrone will develop into a prized landscape specimen. It's a habitat keystone, with springtime clusters of nectar-rich flowers for bees and fleshy fall fruit for birds. The European Strawberry Tree (*A. unedo*) and the selections 'Marina' and 'Compacta' are more garden tolerant and frequently planted in inland gardens.

Attracts bees, butterflies, and hummingbirds; provides food and shelter for birds; larval host for up to 18 moth species.

Pacific Wax Myrtle

Scientific Name *Morella californica*

Family Bayberry (Myricaceae)

Plant Characteristics Erect, rounded, evergreen shrub to small tree with dense, branching foliage, 10–30 feet tall and wide; leaves glossy green, aromatic, lance shaped; flowers tiny, yellow, in dense spikes on stems; fruit tiny, waxy drupes in dense clusters. Deer resistant.

USDA Hardiness Zones 8a–10b

Bloom Period Spring–summer (March–July)

Growing Conditions Full sun, partial shade; sandy, loamy, clayey, moist-to-well-draining soils; water 1x/week in summer once established.

Native to coastal dunes, hills, and conifer woodlands, this densely foliated evergreen can be sheared and shaped as a foundation, border, background hedge, screen, or foliage accent; it can also be pruned into a small to medium-size, multitrunked tree that will accent your patio, courtyard, or entry garden. The ornate foliage is the main garden attraction, except to bees and butterflies, which mob the lackluster flowers, and many birds that devour the small fruit. To increase habitat diversity and seasonal flower color, partner with ceanothus and manzanita selections, California Coffeeberry, Toyon, Hollyleaf Cherry, and currants. Pacific Wax Myrtle thrives in coastal regions, but inland it may need extra summer water and afternoon shade. Also called California Bayberry; the alternate scientific name is *Myrica californica*.

Attracts butterflies, bees, and other pollinators; provides food and shelter for birds; larval host for up to 22 moth species.

Western Redbud

Scientific Name *Cercis occidentalis*

Family Legume (Fabaceae)

Plant Characteristics Deciduous, multitrunked shrub or small tree up to 15 feet tall and wide, with flat-topped, spreading canopy; leaves rounded, 3 inches wide; small flowers red to magenta, dense along bare limbs; fruit a flat, 3-inch pod. Deer resistant.

USDA Hardiness Zones 7a–9b; freezing temps trigger flowering.

Bloom Period Winter–spring (February–April)

Growing Conditions Full sun to partial shade; dry to moist, well-draining soils; water 1–2x/month in summer depending on exposure.

Western Redbud greets spring with a blaze of color. Before the leaves emerge, small, scarlet flowers cover the barren limbs and turn the tree into a fiery beacon that calls to bees and butterflies, which feast on the early-spring buffet. This abundance earns it a place on the top-10 list of important California plants for bees. A rich canopy creates moderate shade, as well as shelter for birds. By summer, brown seed pods, a favorite of seed-eating birds, line the branches. The small stature and spreading canopy suit it for small yards, courtyard accents, entry or pocket gardens, or landscape island accents. Native to shrubby slopes and canyons in chaparral and foothill woodlands, it blooms best in full sun, with winter chill to set the flowers. It is drought tolerant but appreciates extra summer water in hot inland settings. To extend pollinator diversity and seasonal color, pair Western Redbud with ceanothus selections, California Coffeeberry, Blue Elderberry, or Toyon.

Attracts bees, butterflies, and hummingbirds; provides food and shelter for birds; larval host for at least 11 moth species.

Western Spice Bush

Bush Anemone

Shrubs

Chaparral Currant

Lilac Verbena

Golden Yarrow

Blue Witches

Heartleaf Keckiella

Giant Coreopsis

A dominant plant type of all Northern California ecosystems, shrubs should be a primary design element in your pollinator garden. For many shrubs in a Mediterranean climate, the cool, wet winter is their prime season for growth and flowering. Mix early-blooming but summer-deciduous species with late-blooming evergreens to create a year-round flowering and fruiting habitat for bird and insect pollinators.

California Coffeeberry

California Mountain Lilac

Blueblossom

Scientific Name *Ceanothus thyrsiflorus*

Family Buckthorn (Rhamnaceae)

Plant Characteristics Erect, evergreen shrub up to 25 feet tall and wide; leaves oval, bright green, 1–2 inches long; small, blue flowers in dense bundles on stem ends. Palatable to deer.

USDA Hardiness Zones 8b–10b

Bloom Period Winter–spring (February–May)

Growing Conditions Full sun (coastal), partial shade (inland); coarse, well-draining soils; water 1x/month until established, then none; no summer water.

Native from coastal scrub and chaparral to redwood forests, this garden-friendly shrub easily becomes the top celebrity in a pollinator garden. The glamorous flower clusters attract droves of bees and butterflies. Its large size suits it as a specimen accent; a mixed hedge with manzanitas, California Coffeeberry, or California Flannel Bush; or a background anchor for a landscape island surrounded by annuals or perennials like buckwheats, Bush Monkeyflower, and Golden Yarrow. Size and flower color vary in nature, producing excellent cultivars, so choose the ones that are best suited to your garden's size and design. 'Snow Flurry,' with white flowers, reaches 18 feet tall. Mounding 3- to 6-foot-tall selections include the compact 'Skylark,' with dark leaves and bright-blue flowers; 'Arroyo de la Cruz,' with bright-green leaves and light-blue flowers; and 'Big Sur,' also with light-blue flowers. Tip-pruning helps maintain a compact shape.

Attracts butterflies, bees, and other pollinators; larval host for Spring Azure, Echo Blue, Pacuvius Duskywing, California Tortoiseshell, Pale Swallowtail, Hedgerow Hairstreak, and up to 79 other moth and butterfly species.

Blue Witches

Scientific Name *Solanum xanti*

Family Nightshade (Solanaceae)

Plant Characteristics Perennial, multibranched, mounding subshrub 2–3 feet tall and wide; leaves dark green, oval; 1-inch-wide flowers in shades of purple with showy yellow anthers; fruit is a green, pea-size, toxic berry. Deer resistant.

USDA Hardiness Zones 7a–10b

Bloom Period Winter–summer (February–July)

Growing Conditions Full sun, partial shade; sandy, loamy, clayey, well-draining soils; water 1x/month once established.

For much of the year, showy flowers cover this small, mounding plant. Like tomatoes and many other nightshades, the flowers depend on buzz pollination. Bumblebees clasp a bright-yellow stamen column and buzz at a specific frequency that pops it open; then it shoots out a blast of pollen that covers the bee. Use Blue Witches as an informal color accent in wildscape gardens, borders, and fill-ins around patios, or as an attractive container plant. Extra summer water prevents dormancy and loss of leaves. Prune gangly plants in the fall to maintain dense branching. Landscapers often lump this species with the nearly identical *S. parishii* and *S. umbelliferum*. Cultivars such as 'Mountain Pride' and 'Diablo' are available, with flower and foliage color variations. Also called Purple Nightshade and Chaparral Nightshade. *Note:* All parts of the plant are poisonous to humans.

Attracts bees and many other pollinators; birds eat the berries; larval host for up to 35 moth species.

Bush Anemone

Scientific Name *Carpenteria californica*

Family Hydrangea (Hydrangeaceae)

Plant Characteristics Evergreen shrub up to 6 feet tall and wide, open, branching; leathery, dark-green leaves are elliptical, 2–4 inches long; clusters of white flowers are 2–3 inches wide, with showy yellow stamens. Deer resistant.

USDA Hardiness Zones 8a–10b

Bloom Period Spring–summer (May–July)

Growing Conditions Full sun to bright shade (coastal), partial to full shade (inland); deep, loamy, well-draining soils; water 2x/month year-round.

Though rare and endangered—growing on just a few woodland sites in the Sierra Nevada foothills—this adaptable, evergreen shrub happily thrives in home-garden settings. With its dark-green foliage and dense clusters of spectacular, snow-white flowers, it's a show-stopper that makes many top-10 landscape lists for California. Plant Bush Anemone in the shade of a large tree or structure, or use it as a pollinator-garden accent, background, mixed screen, bushy hedge, or patio container specimen. For a four-season pollinator treat, combine with California Coffeeberry, Blue Elderberry, barberries, manzanitas, or currants, or surround a specimen with long-blooming perennials. Prune back the branch tips after blooming to keep the plant compact. In low-rainfall regions, deep watering improves flowering and foliage. The popular 'Elizabeth' cultivar is more vigorous and has larger clusters of flowers.

Attracts butterflies and bees; provides nesting and cover for birds.

Bush Monkeyflower

Scientific Name *Diplacus aurantiacus*

Family Phrymas (Phrymaceae)

Plant Characteristics Evergreen, sprawling subshrub typically 2–4 feet tall and wide, with narrow leaves; paired, 1-inch-long, funnel-shaped flowers are yellow, orange, or red. Deer resistant.

USDA Hardiness Zones 8b–10b

Bloom Period Spring–summer (March–June); fall (depending on environmental factors)

Growing Conditions Partial shade (inland), full sun (coastal); well-draining soils; water 1x/month in spring and summer.

With paired, flamboyant flowers and dense branching and foliage, the versatile and highly variable monkeyflower makes most top-10 lists for Northern California gardens. In the spring, hummingbirds, bees, and sphinx moths flock to the flower buffet; then, after a summer dormancy, the Bush Monkeyflower blooms again. Its small size makes it a good choice for a color accent in a limited-space garden, landscape island, or patio container planting, or a mixed colorscape with salvias, Hummingbird Trumpet, and California Buckwheat. Lightly trimming the spent flower stems will help keep the plant compact. Nurseries carry numerous cultivars with different growth habits and flower colors. Also called Sticky Monkeyflower.

Attracts hummingbirds, hawk moths, solitary bees, carpenter bees, and other insect pollinators; larval host for Chalcedon Checkerspot (Euphydryas chalcedona), Painted Lady (Vanessa virginiensis), and at least 7 other butterfly and moth species.

California Buckwheat

Scientific Name *Eriogonum fasciculatum*

Family Buckwheat (Polygonaceae)

Plant Characteristics Mounding, densely branched, semievergreen subshrub 2–4 feet tall by 3–6 feet wide; leaves needlelike, in fascicles; flowers pink to white, in dense clusters on branch tips; seed heads cinnamon brown. Deer resistant.

USDA Hardiness Zones 7b–10b

Bloom Period Spring–fall (April–September)

Growing Conditions Full sun; coarse, well-draining soils; water 1x/month once established.

Widespread across many vegetation communities, this adaptable, long-blooming buckwheat is blanketed with dense clusters of pinkish to white flowers, followed by rusty-colored seed heads. Plant one in a view garden and enjoy the parade of butterflies and bees from spring through summer, plus seed-eating birds in the fall. For a colorscaped border, background, or informal hedge, combine with manzanitas and ceanothus selections, Bush Monkeyflower, or other mounding shrubs. Four varieties grow through the coastal sage scrub zone from San Diego to Sonoma, and dozens of cultivars have been developed. From sprawling ground covers to small- and medium-size shrubs, with compact to arching branches, choose the one that fits your habitat and garden design. The Xerces Society considers buckwheats to be must-have plants for California habitat gardens.

Highly attractive nectar source for bees and butterflies (especially hairstreaks and blues); birds eat the seeds; larval host for up to 36 species of butterflies and moths.

California Coffeeberry

Scientific Name *Frangula californica*

Family Buckthorn (Rhamnaceae)

Plant Characteristics Evergreen shrub to tree typically 5–10 feet tall and wide; leaves shiny, dark green, elliptical; small, creamy flowers in clusters from leaf axils; fruits in showy drupes ½ inch in diameter, red turning black. Deer resistant.

USDA Hardiness Zones 8a–9b

Bloom Period Summer (June–August)

Growing Conditions Full sun, partial shade; sandy, clayey, loamy, well-draining soils; water 1–2x/month for 1–2 years until established, then no summer water.

Hardy and versatile, California Coffeeberry makes up for its less-than-showy flowers (unless you're a bee!) with ornate fruit and dense foliage. These features make it a superb selection for a pollinator/bird-habitat garden. Use it as a screen or hedge (or smaller cultivars for border shrubs and understory fill-ins) and in a mixed ground cover with small perennials and bunchgrasses. Each of the six subspecies across California has slight geographical differences, allowing propagators to develop numerous cultivars. Choose the tree, shrub, or compact ground cover that best suits your habitat and garden design. The male and female flowers are on different plants, so for fruit you'll need a female with a male nearby. Formerly named *Rhamnus californica*. The related Redberry (*R. crocea*), shrubby and thicket forming, with small leaves, is suitable for hedges and borders.

Attracts bees, butterflies, and other pollinators; provides food, cover, and nesting for birds; larval host for up to 23 butterflies and moths.

California Flannel Bush

Scientific Name *Fremontodendron californicum*

Family Mallow (Malvaceae)

Plant Characteristics Evergreen, mounding to columnar shrub 6–20 feet tall and wide; lobed leaves 3 inches long, covered with irritating hairs; yellow flowers 2–3 inches wide. Deer resistant.

USDA Hardiness Zones 8b–10b

Bloom Period Spring, summer (March–July)

Growing Conditions Full sun; sandy, loamy, well-draining soils; water 1x/month first year until established; no summer water.

With its showy yellow flowers and evergreen leaves, California Flannel Bush is one of California's most spectacular shrubs—but it's easy to love to death with overwatering. Because it's adapted to the dry washes and slopes of chaparral and foothills, wet roots are the kiss of death, especially in the summer. Use it for a background screen, an informal border hedge, or a floral-accent specimen. It pairs well with Blue Elderberry, California Coffeeberry, and ceanothus and manzanita species. Numerous hybrids and cultivars are selected for garden hardiness, size, and floral qualities. The 20-foot tall 'California Glory' is one of the most popular; 'El Dorado Gold' and 'Dara's Gold,' with shiny, green leaves, form 4- to 6-foot-tall mounds. The similar Pine Hill Flannel Bush (*F. decumbens*) reaches 3 feet tall and 6 feet wide. Choose the selection that best meets your garden exposure and water balance, and ensure a dry location.

Attracts butterflies and bees; provides nesting and cover for birds; larval host for the Northern White-Skipper (Heliopetes ericetorum).

California Mountain Lilac

Scientific Name *Ceanothus* 'Concha'

Family Buckthorn (Rhamnaceae)

Plant Characteristics Medium to large, mounding shrub 4–9 feet tall and wide; evergreen leaves narrow, glossy, wrinkled; showy flowers clusters are cobalt blue. Deer resistant.

USDA Hardiness Zones 8a–10b

Bloom Period Spring (March–May)

Growing Conditions Full sun, tolerates partial shade; sandy, clayey, well- to medium-draining soils; no irrigation once established.

Over the decades, this reliable, drought-tolerant hybrid has proved its adaptability in Northern California gardens. Come spring, an explosion of deep-blue flowers covers the arching branches. Used as a midsize background, an informal hedge, a wall screen, or a seasonal accent, it makes a showcase feature for a butterfly garden, and it supplies early-season nectar for Monarchs and Queen bumblebees. Keep it dense by trimming back after spring flowering, as it blooms on cool-season new growth. Other midsize cultivars offer the same landscape features but with slightly different garden requirements: Check out 'Far Horizons,' 'Dark Star,' 'Louis Edmonds,' 'Skylark,' and 'Julia Phelps.' The 'Snowball' cultivar has white flowers.

Attracts hummingbirds, butterflies, and other pollinators; provides nesting and cover for birds; larval host for Spring Azure, Echo Blue, Pacuvius Duskywing, California Tortoiseshell, Pale Swallowtail, and Hedgerow Hairstreak Butterflies.

California Wild Rose

Scientific Name *Rosa californica*

Family Rose (Rosaceae)

Plant Characteristics Deciduous, thicket-forming shrub 3–8 feet tall and wide; canes have hooked thorns; leaves compound, with 5–7 oval, serrated leaflets; flowers pale to dark pink and 1–2 inches wide, with numerous yellow stamens; fruit oval with red hips. Deer resistant.

USDA Hardiness Zones 6a–10b

Bloom Period Spring–summer (April–August)

Growing Conditions Full sun (coastal), partial shade (inland); moist, loamy, well-draining soils; water 1–2x/month in summer.

Widespread across many vegetation communities, California Wild Rose adds high wildlife value to a habitat garden. The arching, prickly branches of this thicket-forming shrub provide excellent shelter, and the gorgeous flowers attract scores of small pollinators. When pruned into a rounded shrub and covered with pink flowers, this wild rose complements a formal poolside or patio garden, or a landscape island. You can also let this aggressive, rhizomatous bush sprawl for a wildscape look as a background, barrier, or wall foundation hedge. For a dramatic contrast, mix it with deciduous plants and evergreens such as Bush Monkeyflower, Golden and Red Currants, California Coffeeberry, Toyon, or California Flannel Bush. Prune to size as severely as needed in winter. Cultivars and hybrids exist, selected for long-blooming flowers with intense color.

Attracts butterflies, bees, and other pollinators; provides cover, nesting for birds; larval host for up to 70 butterflies and moths.

'Canyon Silver' Catalina Silver-Lace

Scientific Name *Constancea nevinii* 'Canyon Silver'

Family Aster (Asteraceae)

Plant Characteristics Rounded, evergreen shrub 3–5 feet tall and wide; leaves silvery white, woolly, deeply cut into lacy, narrow segments; flower heads yellow in flat-topped clusters; seed clusters chocolate brown. Deer resistant.

USDA Hardiness Zones 9b–10b

Bloom Period Spring–fall (April–September)

Growing Conditions Full sun; coarse, well-draining soils; no extra water once established (coastal).

This snow-white horticultural selection, made from a plant endemic to the Channel Islands, is a knockout in a Mediterranean-climate pollinator garden. Tall stems with dense clusters of tiny, lemon-yellow flowers hover over the mound of silvery foliage with a summer-long buffet of pollen and nectar for bees and butterflies. The silvery, eye-catching leaves provides a stunning contrast to glossy evergreen neighbors. For dramatic effect, pair it with Island Bush Poppy, California Coffeeberry, Island Snapdragon, or Giant Coreopsis. Or, for a midgarden highlight, plant it as a year-round foliage accent in a mixed border. Formerly named *Eriophyllum nevinii*.

Attracts butterflies, bees, and other pollinators; birds eat the seeds; larval host for 2 moth species.

Chamise

Scientific Name *Adenostoma fasciculatum*

Family Rose (Rosaceae)

Plant Characteristics Widespread evergreen shrub of the chaparral, 5–15 feet tall and wide; erect to spreading, with a loose matrix of stiff limbs; leaves evergreen, tiny, in bundles, grow along wandlike stems; clusters of small, creamy-white flowers densely cover the branch ends. Deer resistant.

USDA Hardiness Zones 8a–10a

Bloom Period Summer (June–August)

Growing Conditions Full sun; sandy, clayey, coarse, well-draining soils; no summer water once established.

When this member of the rose family bursts into bloom, the bush looks as if it's been hit by a snowstorm. Clusters of small, white flowers obscure the branches and needlelike leaves. Bees and other pollinators visit from dawn to dusk. The informal shrub is best suited for wildscape designs, informal hedges, background accents along a wall or fence, or plantings in naturalized areas. Chamise's extensive root system aids erosion control. Several low-mounting and prostrate cultivars from the Channel Islands make attractive ground covers for rock gardens, borders, fill-in areas, or patio container plantings. Pruning will keep it in bounds and promote vigorous growth. Though it thrives in the hottest, driest chaparral, a bimonthly watering will help keep it lush in the landscape and more fire resistant.

Attracts bees and other insect pollinators; provides shelter and nesting for birds; larval host for up to 18 butterflies and moths.

Chaparral Currant

Scientific Name *Ribes malvaceum*

Family   Gooseberry (Grossulariaceae)

Plant Characteristics Drought-deciduous, multi-stemmed shrub 4–6 feet tall and wide, thornless; leaves lobed to fan shaped, 1–2 inches long; small flowers pinkish to reddish in dangling clusters; fruit a hairy, purple berry. Deer resistant.

USDA Hardiness Zones 7a–10b

Bloom Period Winter–spring (December–April)

Growing Conditions Full sun (coastal), partial shade (inland); coarse, well-draining soils; water 1x/month in summer once established.

Native to coastal chaparral, foothill woodlands from San Francisco to San Diego, and conifer forests of the Northern Coast ranges, this drought-tolerant currant creates a winter wonderland for resident hummingbirds. After losing leaves during the late summer drought, the plant bursts into life with winter rains. The moisture triggers 2- to 6-inch-long hanging clusters of nectar-rich flowers, along with winter color for your habitat garden. By summer, birds feast on the ripe berries. For four-season floral and foliage interest, plant as an understory accent with evergreens like Toyon, California Coffeeberry, and manzanitas and ceanothus selections, or as a floral background, wall or fence border, or screen. Of the two natural varieties, var. *malvaceum* and its cultivars are best suited to Northern California gardens.

Attracts hummingbirds, butterflies, bees and other pollinators; birds eat the berries; larval host for up to 76 butterfly and moth species.

Chaparral Mallow

Scientific Name *Malacothamnus fasciculatus*

Family Mallow (Malvaceae)

Plant Characteristics Spreading, evergreen shrub 3–15 feet tall and wide, with multiple branches; leaves gray, hairy, oval, lobed; flowers pink, 1 inch wide, clustered along stems. Deer resistant.

USDA Hardiness Zones 8b–10b

Bloom Period Spring–summer (April–July)

Growing Conditions Full sun, partial shade; well-draining soils; water 1x/month once established.

Also called Bush Mallow, this widespread native of chaparral and coastal sage scrub communities from the Bay Area south spreads by roots and can form attractive colonies in a wildscape garden setting. Use as a hedge, screen, background along a wall or fence, or fill-in for a sunny corner or slope. Like a miniature hibiscus, one dense bush can display hundreds of pastel-pink flowers in clusters along the softly hairy, gray-green stems. And with a months-long blooming season, it adds rich garden color and keeps pollinators busy from spring through summer. Prune after birds eat the seeds to encourage compact growth. Nurseries carry a number of chaparral mallow varieties and related species that all have similar habitat requirements and garden uses.

Attracts butterflies, bees, hummingbirds; birds eat the seeds; larval host for West Coast Lady (Vanessa annabella), Northern White-Skipper (Heliopetes ericetorum), and at least 2 moth species.

Chokecherry

Scientific Name *Prunus virginiana*

Family Rose (Rosaceae)

Plant Characteristics Deciduous, thicket-forming, multibranched shrub to small tree 3–20 feet tall and wide; leaves glossy green (yellow in fall), oval, 1–4 inches long, with finely toothed edges; small, creamy flowers in elongated clusters 3–6 inches long; fruit a red to black drupe. Deer resistant.

USDA Hardiness Zones 5a–10b

Bloom Period Spring–summer (May–June); fruit: summer

Growing Conditions Full sun, partial shade; moist sandy, loamy, clayey, well-draining soils; water 2x/month in summer.

Spreading by rhizomes, this native of chaparral and open woodlands welcomes wildlife with a feast of flowers, fruit, and foliage. Soon after spring leaves emerge, long tassels of pollen and nectar-rich flowers entice bees, the primary pollinators, and butterflies. Come summer birds flock to devour the fleshy drupes, and the shiny green leaves host numerous butterfly and moth caterpillars. This garden-friendly pollinator keystone adds three-season beauty well into the fall when the leaves turn gold and red. Use as an accent shrub in a habitat island, understory fill-in, background screen, or hedge, or prune into a small tree for limited spaces. It partners well with Common Snowberry, California Wild Rose, Red Osier Dogwood, and currants. Cultivars with green leaves that age to purple then turn red in autumn include 'Schubert,' a suckering tree, and 'Canada Red' which doesn't sucker.

Attracts bees, butterflies, and other pollinators; provides shelter and food for birds; larval host for Western Tiger Swallowtail (Papilio rutulus), Ceanothus Silkmoth (Hyalophora euryalus), and up to 122 other butterfly and moth species.

Cleveland Sage

Scientific Name *Salvia clevelandii*

Family Mint (Lamiaceae)

Plant Characteristics Rounded, evergreen shrub 3–5 feet tall and wide; gray-green leaves lance shaped, 3 inches long, highly aromatic; blue flowers tubular, in whorls on 1-foot-long spikes. Deer resistant.

USDA Hardiness Zones 8a–10b

Bloom Period Spring–summer (April–July)

Growing Conditions Full sun; sandy, gravelly, well-draining soils; water 1x/month in summer until established.

Loved as the most fragrant sage, this garden standout becomes Grand Central Station when spikes of sky-blue flowers blanket the shrub. The whorls of tubular flowers floating above the gray-green foliage create a dazzling buffet for hummingbirds, bees, and all other insect pollinators, and the aromatic leaves will perfume your entire yard. Ideal for perimeter color, a midgarden focus, low hedges, ground covers, patio accents, or container plants. To increase color and habitat diversity, integrate with Bush Monkeyflower, Hummingbird Trumpet, and California Buckwheat. Prune back mature plants by one-third to encourage dense foliage, flowering, and compact structure. Many easy-to-grow cultivars and hybrids are suitable for Northern California, so choose one that fits your habitat and design; hardy 'Winnifred Gilman' and 'Allen Chickering' are popular garden selections.

Attracts hummingbirds, butterflies, bees; birds eat the seeds; larval host for up to 6 moth species.

Common Snowberry

Scientific Name *Symphoricarpos albus* var. *laevigatus*

Family Honeysuckle (Caprifoliaceae)

Plant Characteristics Rounded, branching, deciduous shrub 3–6 feet tall and wide, thicket forming; leaves blue-green, oval, 1–2 inches long; flowers small, pinkish white, bell shaped, in short, tight clusters; fruit a pearl-size white drupe. Deer resistant.

USDA Hardiness Zones 5a–9b

Bloom Period Spring–summer (May–July); fruit: fall–winter

Growing Conditions Full sun, partial shade; coarse, loamy, or clayey, well-drained soils; water 1–3x/month once established.

Native to mountains and foothill woodlands, this spreading, thicket-forming shrub develops dense branches with arching stems in full sun, but it also easily nestles beneath trees. Hummingbirds and bees love the pink flowers, and birds find shelter in the dense branches, but the real garden highlight comes in the winter when dense clusters of marble-size, snow-white drupes dangle on the limbs. Plant Common Snowberry as a hedge, background, mixed border, or understory accent. Partner with Toyon, California Coffeeberry, currants, gooseberries, and California Wild Rose. Spreads by rhizomes; shear to size in winter, or severely prune to rejuvenate. The low-growing Creeping Snowberry (*S. mollis*) thrives in coastal gardens and oak woodlands.

Attracts butterflies, bees, hummingbirds, and other pollinators; provides food and shelter for birds; larval host for checkerspot butterflies (Euphydryas spp.) and up to 28 moth species.

Coyote Brush

Scientific Name *Baccharis pilularis* ssp. *pilularis*
  'Pigeon Point'

Family Aster (Asteraceae)

Plant Characteristics Low, sprawling subshrub with
  leafy stems 2–3 feet tall, 6–9 feet wide; evergreen, oval
  leaves, ½ inch long; tiny male and female flowers on
  different plants; seeds in fluffy plumes. Deer resistant.

USDA Hardiness Zones 7b–10b

Bloom Period Fall–winter (October–January)

Growing Conditions Full sun; sandy to clayey, well-draining soils;
  water 1–2x/month in summer once established.

In nature, Coyote Brush comes in two sizes. The erect, shrubby subspecies *consanguinea* reaches 3–12 feet tall, while the coastal subspecies *pilularis* hugs the ground. 'Pigeon Point' and many other cultivars have been selected as premier evergreen ground covers. Most cultivars are male plants that don't produce fluffy seed masses, but the inconspicuous flowers still pack a nectar-rich punch for hordes of insect pollinators. The dense branching provides excellent cover for ground-foraging birds. Both types respond well to moderate shaping and severe pruning. Prune shrubby Coyote Brush as a dense, 3- to 6-foot-tall natural or formal hedge or background shrub. Annually trim the ground cover to maintain a dense mound. For complete cover in 2 years, plant 'Pigeon Point' on 6- to 10-foot centers. Use it as a walkway border, or mix with other low-growing color accents such as ceanothus species, Hummingbird Trumpet, Spreading Coastal Gumplant, and Golden Yarrow.

Attracts butterflies, bees, and other insect pollinators; provides cover for birds; larval host for up to 18 moth species.

Cream Bush

Scientific Name *Holodiscus discolor*

Family Rose (Rosaceae)

Plant Characteristics Deciduous, multistemmed shrub to small tree 5–18 feet tall and wide, with slender, arching branches; leaves gray-green, oval, 1–3 inches long, with toothed margins; small, creamy flowers form dense, pyramidal sprays 4–10 inches long and wide on branch tips; seeds tiny, wind dispersed. Deer resistant.

USDA Hardiness Zones 5b–10a

Bloom Period Spring–summer (May–August)

Growing Conditions Partial shade, tolerates shade; coarse, gravelly, loamy, well-draining soils; water 2x/month once established; needs summer water.

Common to forest openings and understories, this fast-growing shrub thrives in partial shade. In the spring, its spectacular clusters of creamy flowers are butterfly magnets and eye-catching garden accents. Heavy with frothy flowers, the branches usually droop, giving the plant its other common name, Ocean Spray. It adds fall color with yellow to red leaves. Use in backgrounds, as an understory accent, along walls or walkways, or in mixed plantings. It complements currants, Oregon Grape, and California Wild Rose, and works well as a fill-in color accent with Western Mock Orange, Red Osier Dogwood, California Bay, or 'Howard McMinn' Manzanita. Prune occasionally after flowering to maintain a loose, graceful shrub, and trim off the spent brown flower clusters for a manicured look.

Attracts butterflies, bees, and other insect pollinators; provides shelter for birds; larval host for up to 37 butterfly and moth species.

Dr. Hurd Manzanita

Scientific Name *Arctostaphylos manzanita* 'Dr. Hurd'

Family Heath (Ericaceae)

Plant Characteristics Large, evergreen, treelike shrub 10–15 feet tall and wide, with attractive reddish-brown bark; leaves oval, gray-green; flowers white, urn shaped, in small clusters; fruit ⅜ inch in diameter, with reddish berries. Deer resistant.

USDA Hardiness Zones 8a–10b

Bloom Period Winter–spring (January–March)

Growing Conditions Full sun; well-draining, sandy, loamy, clayey soils; water 1x/month in summer once established.

With multiple ornate trunks; colorful, smooth-skinned bark; evergreen foliage; and showy flower clusters and fruit, manzanita species are prized contributors to a pollinator garden. Fast growing and garden tolerant, this tree-size hybrid thrives in Northern California landscapes. Bees are the primary pollinators, and the flowers provide a seasonal nectar source for hummingbirds. It makes a dynamic visual accent as a specimen tree or tall anchor surrounded by small shrubs or ground covers. For companion plants, select shrubs and perennials native to your specific area, such as California Flannel Bush, Hollyleaf Cherry, California Coffeeberry, and ceanothus selections. Nurseries carry numerous manzanita cultivars and hybrids, so be sure to choose one suitable for your area and landscape design.

Attracts bees, butterflies, hummingbirds; provides food and shelter for birds; larval host for up to 54 moth species.

Fragrant Sumac

Scientific Name *Rhus aromatica*

Family Sumac (Anacardaceae)

Plant Characteristics Spreading, deciduous, multi-branched, rhizomatous shrub with stems 3–6 feet tall and wide; leaves compound with 3 leaflets, pungent, orange in fall; flowers not showy; fruit in clusters of sticky, red drupes. Deer resistant.

USDA Hardiness Zones 5b–10b

Bloom Period Spring (March–May); fruit: July–October

Growing Conditions Best in full sun, tolerates partial shade; coarse, well-draining soils; water 1x/month once established.

Native to chaparral, coastal sage scrub, and inner mountain eco-systems, this widespread shrub provides three seasons of premier pollinator benefits and garden colorscaping. The tiny, yellow flowers are inconspicuous, except to the bees that dive in for an all-important early-spring source of nectar. Clusters of ornamental red fruit decorate the compact shrub in the summer and feed the birds. Come autumn, the leaves turn hues of orange and red for a burst of brilliant garden color. Partner it with flowering evergreens as a foliage accent for borders, background hedges, or slope plantings. Waist-high "low-grow" cultivars are available for walkway borders or medians. Male and female sumac plants are separate, so you'll need both to get fruit. Prune to size in the winter to keep it compact and dense.

Attracts bees and butterflies; provides seeds and shelter for birds; larval host for up to 20 moth species.

Fuchsia-Flowered Gooseberry

Scientific Name *Ribes speciosum*

Family Gooseberry (Grossulariaceae)

Plant Characteristics Winter- and summer deciduous shrub 4–6 feet tall and wide, with multiple thorny stems for the base; leaves waxy green, rounded, lobed; scarlet, tubular flowers dangle from the leaf axils all along the stems; berries red. Deer resistant.

USDA Hardiness Zones 8a–10b

Bloom Period Winter–spring (January–May)

Growing Conditions Partial shade, tolerates full sun (coastal); sandy, clayey, well-draining soils; water 1–2x/month until established.

Its long, arching stems lined with dangling scarlet flowers, this thorny currant is a winter–spring celebrity in a wildlife habitat garden. It supplies winter nectar for hummingbirds, spring flowers for bees and butterflies, and summer fruit for birds. Then it goes dormant, with no leaves for several months, revealing thorny stems covered with red berries. By New Year's, it's back in all its glory. For four-season color and pollinator diversity, partner it with evergreens such as California Bay, Hollyleaf Cherry, or Pacific Wax Myrtle. It's a colorful accent against the evergreen foliage of Toyon or California Coffeeberry. To shield from human contact and accentuate its arching stems, plant it in a raised garden or as a color highlight in a landscape island. Prune or thin after the fruit is gone. Nurseries sell numerous cultivars, so be sure to choose one that matches your habitat and design.

Attracts hummingbirds, butterflies, and bees; birds eat the berries; larval host for up to 80 butterfly and moth species.

Giant Coreopsis

Scientific Name *Coreopsis gigantea*

Family Aster (Asteraceae)

Plant Characteristics Erect, summer-deciduous shrub 3–6 feet tall, sparsely branched, crown rounded; leaves bright green, filament-like, clustered on branch tips; flowers daisylike, 3 inches wide, with yellow rays, orange disks. Deer and rabbit resistant when mature, palatable when young.

USDA Hardiness Zones 9b–10a

Bloom Period Winter–spring (January–May)

Growing Conditions Full sun; sandy, well-draining soils; no summer water and no water once established.

With a bare base; shaggy clusters of bright-green, hairlike leaves on the branch tips; and crowned with clusters of large, yellow, daisylike flowers, this bizarre plant is a showstopper. Native to the Channel Islands and Santa Monica Mountains, the plant grows best near the coast. It loses its glory during summer, when the foliage dies; then it bursts back to life with winter rains. Resist trying to delay summer dormancy, as extra water is the kiss of death. To maintain summer garden color and pollinator resources, mix with California Buckwheat, Island Snapdragon, Bush Monkeyflower, and Seaside Daisy. Plant this dramatic floral accent in nonirrigated garden spots or habitat islands, or use as a poolside or patio container accent. Easy to grow from seed. Also named *Leptosyne gigantea*.

Attracts bees, butterflies, and other insect pollinators; larval host for up to 5 moth species.

Golden Currant

Scientific Name *Ribes aureum*

Family Gooseberry (Grossulariaceae)

Plant Characteristics Winter-deciduous shrub 3–6 feet tall and wide, with multiple, thornless stems from base; leaves pale-green, rounded, with 3 lobes; flowers yellow, tubular, clustered in leaf axils along branches; berries red, orange, or black. Deer resistant.

USDA Hardiness Zones 5a–10b

Bloom Period Spring–summer (April–June)

Growing Conditions Full sun (coastal), partial shade (inland); fine to coarse, loamy, well-draining soils; water 1–2x/month in summer.

With fragrant, golden-yellow early-spring flowers and abundant summer berries, this plant has exceptional high wildlife value, especially for hummingbirds, songbirds, and Monarch Butterflies. Add its ornate, lobed leaves that turn hues of burgundy in the fall, and you have a premier addition to your pollinator garden. Currants spread by rhizomes and can form a thick background against a wall, along a border, or as an understory fill-in. They accent an oval garden, courtyard, or poolside, or they can be trimmed into a well-foliated container plant. They occur naturally along streams, so summer water keeps them robust, and fall pruning maintains the desired size and dense branching. Nurseries carry several varieties and cultivars. The *gracillimum* variety is best to use from coast to foothills.

Attracts hummingbirds, butterflies, bumblebees, long-tongued bees; birds eat the berries; larval host for up to 80 butterflies and moths.

Golden Yarrow

Scientific Name *Eriophyllum confertiflorum*

Family Aster (Asteraceae)

Plant Characteristics Erect, semievergreen subshrub 1–2 feet tall and wide, with multiple woolly stems; leaves silvery green with narrow lobes; yellow flower heads form dense, rounded clusters. Deer resistant.

USDA Hardiness Zones 7b–11a

Bloom Period Winter–summer (January–August)

Growing Conditions Full sun; well-draining soils; water 2x/month once established.

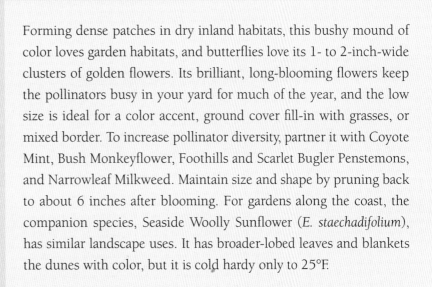

Forming dense patches in dry inland habitats, this bushy mound of color loves garden habitats, and butterflies love its 1- to 2-inch-wide clusters of golden flowers. Its brilliant, long-blooming flowers keep the pollinators busy in your yard for much of the year, and the low size is ideal for a color accent, ground cover fill-in with grasses, or mixed border. To increase pollinator diversity, partner it with Coyote Mint, Bush Monkeyflower, Foothills and Scarlet Bugler Penstemons, and Narrowleaf Milkweed. Maintain size and shape by pruning back to about 6 inches after blooming. For gardens along the coast, the companion species, Seaside Woolly Sunflower (*E. staechadifolium*), has similar landscape uses. It has broader-lobed leaves and blankets the dunes with color, but it is cold hardy only to 25°F.

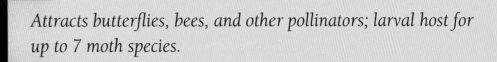

Attracts butterflies, bees, and other pollinators; larval host for up to 7 moth species.

Heartleaf Keckiella

Scientific Name *Keckiella cordifolia*

Family Plantain (Plantaginaceae)

Plant Characteristics Rounded, sprawling, semi-evergreen subshrub, typically 1–3 feet tall and wide, with trailing, vinelike branches; paired, glossy, heart-shaped leaves, 1–3 inches long; flowers tubular, 1–2 inches long, red to pale orange, in clusters from leaf axils. Deer resistant.

USDA Hardiness Zones 6b–10a

Bloom Period Spring–summer (May–July)

Growing Conditions Full sun (coastal), partial shade (inland); well-draining soils; irrigate 1x/month once established, tolerates summer water.

This chaparral plant with clusters of flamboyant flowers forces you to make decisions. You can trim it back in late summer to 1 foot to keep it compact and bushy or let it spread with rooting stems and root shoots as a ground cover. Other options are to let the sprawling branches reach 6–8 feet long and droop over a retaining wall, boulder, or slope; arch over a wall or fence; or intertwine with other shrubs. To add garden color and pollinator diversity, mix with California Buckwheat, Cleveland Sage, Bush Monkeyflower, or currants. Native to the coast and coastal mountains, where it's evergreen, it loses its leaves with freezing temperatures and in the hot summers of inland areas unless given extra water. Also called Red Climbing Penstemon.

Pollinated by hummingbirds; attracts butterflies, bees; provides shelter and seeds for birds; larval host for Chalcedon Checkerspot Butterflies (Euphydryas chalcedona).

Howard McMinn Manzanita

Scientific Name *Arctostaphylos densiflora* 'Howard McMinn'

Family Heath (Ericaceae)

Plant Characteristics Evergreen, mounding shrub with red bark and twisting branches 6–10 feet tall and wide; leaves shiny green, lance shaped, 1-inch long; flowers white to pinkish, urn shaped, in dense clusters on branch tips; fruit small, reddish berries. Deer resistant.

USDA Hardiness Zones 7a–10b

Bloom Period Winter–spring (February–April)

Growing Conditions Full sun (coastal), partial shade (inland); coarse, well-draining soils; water 1x/month max in summer once established.

This medium-size cultivar is one of the most garden-hardy manzanitas available. Derived from the rare and endangered Vine Hill Manzanita, it creates its own pollinator supermarket. The showy clusters of bell-shaped flowers provide early-season nectar for Queen bumblebees to build their nest colonies. Birds eat the berries, and the foliage and intricate branching provide cover and nesting sites. When trimmed up, the sinuous, red-barked limbs, accented with shiny, evergreen leaves and a spring blanket of flowers, create a dazzling specimen. Use it as a landscape focal point or with a mixed planting of ceanothus species, Bush Monkeyflower, Toyon, or California Flannel Bush. It prunes well to size as a dense shrub, garden background, border, or retaining wall accent. Nurseries carry numerous cultivars and hybrids, so be sure to choose one suitable for your habitat and garden design.

Attracts bees, butterflies, hummingbirds, and other pollinators; provides cover and food for birds; larval host for up to 48 species of moths.

Hummingbird Trumpet

Scientific Name *Epilobium canum*

Family Evening primrose (Onagraceae)

Plant Characteristics Low-growing, branching, deciduous subshrub 6–24 inches tall and wide; gray-green leaves narrow, pointed, in bundles on stems; flowers funnel shaped, scarlet, in spikelike clusters. Deer resistant.

USDA Hardiness Zones 7a–10b

Bloom Period Summer–fall (August–September)

Growing Conditions Full sun; well-draining soils; water 1x/ month (inland).

Considered a premier hummingbird plant and on every top-10 list, the long-blooming Hummingbird Trumpet adds eye-catching pop as a spreading ground cover, a landscape island or rock-garden accent, a foreground or walkway border, or a poolside or courtyard container plant. Plant it in a view garden, and enjoy the hummingbird circus. Unlike many plants that flower in the spring and go dormant in the dry summer, this plant blooms in the late summer to coincide with the hummingbird southern migration. For three-season color, combine with Bush Monkeyflower, Hummingbird Sage and other salvias, and penstemon species. Encourage dense spring growth by cutting back to the ground in the winter after the flowers are spent. Several other *Epilobium* species and numerous cultivars offer a variety of sizes reaching 5 feet tall, with foliage ranging in color from silver to bright green and flowers ranging from scarlet to pink to orange, so pick the one that best suits your garden design. Spreads by rhizomes and readily self-seeds. Also called California Fuchsia and Zauschneria.

Highly attractive to hummingbirds, butterflies, bees, sphinx moths; larval host for up to 15 species of moths.

Island Bush Poppy

Scientific Name *Dendromecon harfordii*

Family Poppy (Papaveraceae)

Plant Characteristics Evergreen, mounding shrub to small tree, typically 5–10 feet tall and wide; leaves soft green, elliptical, 2–3 inches long, with rounded tips; abundant yellow flowers 3 inches wide. Palatable to deer.

USDA Hardiness Zones 7b–10a

Bloom Period Spring–summer (March–July)

Growing Conditions Full sun–partial shade; coarse, well-draining soils; water plants in full sun 1x/month in summer once established.

Native to the Channel Islands in chaparral, sage scrub, and woodland canyons, this spectacular selection adapts well to garden settings. The gray-green, evergreen leaves and brilliant yellow flowers make Island Bush Poppy an eye-catching standout. The flowers burst into glory in the spring, then can keep blooming throughout much of the year. It's a delightful floral accent as a specimen, garden background, wall screen, border, or hedge. For a mixed-plant colorscape, combine with Hollyleaf Cherry, medium-size ceanothus species, Island Snapdragon, or Bush Monkeyflower. Also called Channel Island Tree Poppy. The less ornamental Bush Poppy (*D. rigida*) is widespread in the Coast Ranges and Sierra foothills. It has erect stems and a shorter spring bloom season, and similar landscape requirements and uses.

Attracts bees, butterflies, and other insect pollinators; larval host for at least 1 moth species.

Island Snapdragon

Scientific Name *Gambelia speciosa*

Family Plantain (Plantaginaceae)

Plant Characteristics Mounding, evergreen shrub with dense, arching stems 3–4 feet tall, 5–7 feet wide; leaves small, light green, oval, whorled; tubular red flowers in 1-inch-long clusters on branch tips. Deer resistant.

USDA Hardiness Zones 9a–10b

Bloom Period Winter–summer (February–June)

Growing Conditions Full sun, partial shade (inland); well-draining soils; water 1–2x/month once established.

With arching branches tipped with clusters of scarlet flowers, this Channel Islands import adapts well to pollinator gardens and provides a rich nectar buffet for hummingbirds and butterflies. Plant it as an accent or focal point of a view garden, and enjoy the show. Use in a mixed border or midgarden accent, on a retaining wall or trellis to emphasize the arching stems, or in a patio container. To maintain a late-summer nectar source and sustained garden color, partner with California Buckwheat, Malva Rosa, Island Bush Poppy, or Bush Monkeyflower. The cultivar 'Bocarosa' has bright-green leaves, while 'Firecracker' has hairy leaves. Trim back as needed to maintain shape and size; prune to ground in winter to rejuvenate. If not trimmed, the long branches tend to trail up through other shrubs for an interesting mix of textures and colors. Previously named *Galvezia speciosa*.

Attracts hummingbirds, butterflies, and other insect pollinators.

Lilac Verbena

Scientific Name *Verbena lilacina*

Family Verbena (Verbenaceae)

Plant Characteristics Mounding, evergreen subshrub 2–3 feet tall and wide; leaves deeply divided into narrow segments; flowers ½ inch wide, dark purple, in 1-inch spherical clusters on stem tips. Deer resistant.

USDA Hardiness Zones 7a–10b

Bloom Period Spring–fall (March–October, inland); year-round (coastal)

Growing Conditions Full sun, tolerates partial shade; coarse, well-draining soils; water 1–2x/month in summer (inland).

With a Mediterranean climate like that of coastal California, Cedros Island, off the Mexican coast, is part of the California Floristic Province, and many of its plants easily adapt to mainland landscapes. The exceptional Lilac Verbena cultivar 'De La Mina' is fast growing, drought tolerant, densely foliated, and covered with clusters of vibrant purple blooms nearly year-round. The mounds of color brighten walkway borders, garden foregrounds, boulder accents, and containers for courtyards and patios. The long blooming season provides a dependable nectar-rich buffet for butterflies and bees, so plant it where you can enjoy the fluttering visitors. Extra summer water in inland gardens extends blooming. Prune back about one-third once a year to keep it dense, and a little trim after the spring bloom will encourage summer flowers.

Attracts butterflies, bees, and other pollinators; larval host for Common Buckeye (Junonia coenia) and up to 6 moth species.

Malva Rosa

Scientific Name *Malva assurgentiflora*

Family Mallow (Malvaceae)

Plant Characteristics Sprawling-to-mounding, multi-branched, evergreen shrub 6–12 feet tall and wide; leaves rounded with 5–7 triangular lobes; flowers 2–3 inches wide, petals magenta to pink with dark lines. Palatable to deer and gophers.

USDA Hardiness Zones 9a–10b

Bloom Period Winter–summer, fall (February–July, September–October)

Growing Conditions Full sun; sandy, loamy, well-draining soils; water 1–2x/month, including summer.

This rare tree mallow has almost been grazed out of existence in the coastal bluffs and sage scrub of the Channel Islands, but it thrives in coastal gardens and a few naturalized areas on the coast. In your habitat garden, the bright, eye-catching flowers will attract a stream of butterfly, bee, and hummingbird visitors. With maplelike leaves and flamboyant, almost-year-round flowers, it makes an attractive informal evergreen hedge, screen, or garden background. You can trim it up as a small tree or prune it to keep it dense as a rounded specimen shrub for a walkway, courtyard garden accent, or container plant. For colorscaping companion plants, it pairs well with Bush Monkeyflower, Island Bush Poppy, St. Catherine's Lace and other buckwheats, and California Goldenrod. Also known as Island (or Tree) Mallow.

Attracts butterflies, bees, and hummingbirds; provides seeds and cover for birds; larval host for Painted Lady (Vanessa cardui) and up to 14 other butterfly and moth species.

115

Naked Buckwheat

Scientific Name *Eriogonum nudum*

Family Buckwheat (Polygonaceae)

Plant Characteristics Perennial, evergreen subshrub with basal rosette 3–6 inches tall and wide; slender, leafless, branching flower stems 2–5 feet tall; small flowers in spherical clusters are white, sometimes pink or yellow. Deer resistant.

USDA Hardiness Zones 5b–10b

Bloom Period Spring–summer (May–August)

Growing Conditions Full sun (coastal), partial shade (inland); sandy, coarse, well-draining soils; water 1x/month in summer once established.

With 14 varieties, this flower with waist-high stems fills environmental niches statewide, so nursery selections are naturally garden hardy. The slender, leafless (naked) stems divide repeatedly to create a 2-foot-wide cloud of pom-pom-like flower clusters that attract clouds of pollinators, especially in the summer, when many flowers have faded. Use as a color accent, or, for a dramatic colorscape and pollinator buffet, mass-plant a border or background with California Buckwheat, penstemon species, Hummingbird Trumpet, Bush Monkeyflower, or Yarrow in varied color selections. The cultivar 'Ella Nelson's Yellow' has brilliant yellow flowers. Acmon Blue and other butterflies feast on the nectar, then lay their eggs on the basal leaves. The caterpillars overwinter in leaf litter, so leave your garden a little wild to protect them.

Attracts butterflies, bees, and many other pollinators; birds eat the seeds; larval host for Acmon Blue (Plebejus acmon), Mormon Metalmark (Apodemia mormo), and up to 48 other butterfly and moth species.

Oregon Grape

Scientific Name *Berberis aquifolium*

Family Barberry (Berberidaceae)

Plant Characteristics Upright, evergreen shrub 3–6 feet tall; compound leaves have 5–9 glossy, hollylike leaflets lined with prickles; flowers small, golden yellow, in dense clusters, followed by bluish-purple, ⅜-inch-diameter fruit. Deer resistant.

USDA Hardiness Zones 6a–8b

Bloom Period Spring (March–May)

Growing Conditions Partial sun to full shade; moist, loamy soils; water 1x/month, 2x/month in summer.

Native to open woods and shrublands, this evergreen fills the bill for a shade-tolerant understory plant with year-round appeal as a beautiful garden component and a wildlife-friendly plant. Early-spring flowers attract pollinators; birds feast on the summer fruit. With thick, glossy, evergreen leaves and dense branching, barberries are excellent as specimens, accents, borders, and barrier and foundation plantings. The leaves of some selections turn purplish bronze in the winter. Nurseries offer a number of cultivars and hybrids. The mainstay 'Golden Abundance' can reach 8 feet tall and wide. The cultivar 'Compacta' and the native Longleaf Barberry (*B. nervosa*) top out at 3 feet, ideal for ground covers or low borders. Creeping Barberry (*B. repens*), at 4–6 inches tall, is shade adapted and spreads by rhizomes.

Attracts bees and other pollinators; provides food, nesting sites for birds; larval host for at least 5 moth species.

Our Lord's Candle

Scientific Name *Hesperoyucca whipplei*

Family Asparagus (Asparagaceae)

Plant Characteristics Trunkless with a dense rosette of narrow, sharp-pointed, spearlike leaves ¾ inch wide, 1–3 feet long; flowering stalk grows 8–10 feet tall, with branching clusters of creamy flowers; after 5–10 years, the plant blooms and dies. Deer resistant.

USDA Hardiness Zones 8b–10a

Bloom Period Spring (April–May)

Growing Conditions Performs best in full sun, tolerates mild shade; dry, rocky, clayey, well-draining soils. No summer water once established.

Also appropriately called Chaparral Yucca, this yucca relative is common on chaparral and coastal sage scrub slopes in the Mediterranean climate and desert regions from Monterey to San Diego. The 3- to 4-foot-wide rosettes lend a bold presence to any garden and need ample space to mature. After years of providing evergreen texture, the mounding rosette bursts into bloom, with a towering stalk flagged with showy clusters of white flowers, and then the plant dies. Before blooming, the bushlike rosette makes a dominant ground cover and pairs well with Chamise, Coyote Brush, and California Buckwheat. Like other yuccas, the flowers depend on a single species of small, white moth for pollination. Easily propagated from seed and grows moderately fast.

Attracts Tegeticula maculata *moths for pollination; provides nesting sites for thrashers and other desert birds; larval host for up to 6 species of moths and butterflies.*

Pacific Ninebark

Scientific Name *Physocarpus capitatus*

Family Rose (Rosaceae)

Plant Characteristics Deciduous, erect shrub
3–8 feet tall and 5 feet wide; multiple stems have
peeling bark; leaves are maplelike, orange in fall,
1–3 inches long, with 3–5 lobes; small, white
flowers in spherical clusters 3–5 inches wide,
fruit a cluster of red capsules. Deer resistant.

USDA Hardiness Zones 5a–10b

Bloom Period Spring–summer (May–June)

Growing Conditions Full sun, partial shade; moist, clayey, loamy,
sandy, medium- to well-draining soils; water 1x/month in summer
once established.

Native to forests and open woodlands in the Northern Coast ranges
and Sierras, this attractive native offers four-season beauty for a woodland garden palette. Spring brings masses of dense flowers loved by
bees and butterflies; in summer, the leafy branches provide shelter for
birds and clusters of glossy-red seed capsules. Then, in fall, the leaves
turn brilliant hues of reddish orange, followed in winter by arching,
bare stems with ornate, shredding bark. Use Pacific Ninebark as an
understory wildscape accent or as a garden background, wall border,
screen, or hedge planting. Pairs well with other woodland plants like
Red Osier Dogwood, currants, Chokecherry, Cream Bush, and Western Spirea. Prune in winter to maintain size, shape, and dense foliage.

*Attracts bees, butterflies, and other pollinators; provides shelter and
seeds for birds.*

Pink-Flowering Currant

Scientific Name *Ribes sanguineum* var. *glutinosum*

Family Gooseberry (Grossulariaceae)

Plant Characteristics Deciduous shrub 6–10 feet tall, with multiple stems; leaves rounded, lobed, 3 inches wide; flowers pink to rose, tubular, in dense, dangling 6-inch-long clusters; fruit a black berry. Deer resistant.

USDA Hardiness Zones 8b–10b

Bloom Period Winter–spring (February–April)

Growing Conditions Partial shade; coarse to clayey, well-draining soils; summer water 1–3x/month in dry inland region.

Fast growing, with flamboyant red flowers and succulent berries, this currant is a wildlife supermarket. Flowering starts in the winter, when hummingbirds critically need a nectar source; the plant feeds Monarch Butterflies through the spring, and songbirds feast on the berries all summer. In a mixed planting, the dangling clusters of brilliant flowers really bounce against the evergreen foliage of Toyon, California Coffeeberry, or Hollyleaf Cherry. You can also use Pink-Flowering Currant as a background or floral accent against a wall or walkway, or to highlight a semishaded corner. Provide extra summer water in inland regions, and prune to shape if needed after fruiting. Though it is native from coastal Santa Barbara northward, there are also many garden-friendly cultivars, so choose one suited to your garden habitat and design.

Attracts hummingbirds, butterflies, and bees; birds eat the berries; larval host for up to 80 butterflies and moths.

Red Osier Dogwood

Scientific Name *Cornus sericea*

Family Dogwood (Cornaceae)

Plant Characteristics Deciduous shrub with multiple wandlike stems 3–10 feet tall, leafless stems turn red in winter; leaves bright green, oval, 2–4 inches long, tips pointed; small, white flowers form showy clusters; fruit is clusters of small, white drupes. Palatable to deer.

USDA Hardiness Zones 5a–10b

Bloom Period Spring–summer (April–June)

Growing Conditions Partial to full shade; moist, loamy, medium- to slow-draining soils; water 1x/week once established.

This open-branching plant naturally grows as an understory shrub along streams, so in a habitat garden it thrives in dappled shade and regular irrigation. Make it happy, and it will provide year-round color and three seasons of forage and cover for wildlife. In the spring, bees, butterflies, and moths feast on the showy clusters of creamy flowers; then, come summer, birds devour the fleshy, white drupes. The dense foliage provides nesting and shelter for birds, but that's not all. The ornate leaves turn hues of yellow and orange in the fall, then drop to reveal a multistemmed matrix of red branches that provide a vivid color accent all winter. Use as a background plant; wall screen; landscape island anchor; or year-round color accent for patios, courtyards, and poolsides. It spreads by rhizomes and can form colonies in loose garden soil. Also called Creek and American Dogwood.

Attracts butterflies, bees, moths, and other insects; birds eat the fruit; larval host for up to 42 moth species.

Salal

Scientific Name *Gaultheria shallon*

Family Heath (Ericaceae)

Plant Characteristics Spreading, evergreen, rhizomatous shrub 2–5 feet tall and wide; leaves elliptical, leathery, 2–4 inches long; small flowers urn shaped, white to pinkish, 5–15 on one-sided, spikelike array; fruit purple, berrylike, fleshy, ⅜ inch in diameter. Deer resistant.

USDA Hardiness Zones 8a–10b

Bloom Period Spring (April–May); fruit: July–September

Growing Conditions Partial sun to full shade; rich, humous, well-draining soils; water 2x/month in summer.

This understory shrub thrives in coastal and northern conifer forests, sometimes spreading to form dense thickets, so it's well suited for a woodland-palette habitat garden. Give it partial shade and ample summer water, and in the spring its striking flowers will provide abundant pollen and nectar for small insects. In the summer, the juicy berries feed the birds, and the dense foliage offers cover to birds and wildlife all year. In sun it grows as a ground cover to subshrub 1–3 feet tall, while in shade it can develop into a dense 5x5-foot shrub suitable for a hedge, screen, or understory fill-in. Partner it with forest companions like Western Azalea, Red Osier Dogwood, Cream Bush, Pacific Ninebark, currants, and Western Mock Orange. The floral industry widely uses the attractive, dark-green leaves in flower arrangements.

Attracts hummingbirds and small insects; excellent food and shelter source for birds; larval host for the Brown Elfin Butterfly (Callophrys augustinus) *and up to 3 moth species.*

Santa Cruz Island Buckwheat

Scientific Name *Eriogonum arborescens*

Family Buckwheat (Polygonaceae)

Plant Characteristics Mounding to spreading, evergreen shrub 2–4 feet tall and slightly wider; leaves pale green to gray, narrow, 1–2 inches long, in tight whorls; flowers small, light pink to white, in dense clusters on branch tips; reddish-brown seed heads in fall. Deer resistant.

USDA Hardiness Zones 7b–10b

Bloom Period Spring–fall (April–October)

Growing Conditions Full sun; well-draining soils; water 1x/month once established.

With dense whorls of slender leaves and flat-topped clusters of lacy, pink-and-white flowers, this elegant mound of color forms an eye-catching accent in gardens, especially for pollinators. This keystone, nectar-rich "supermarket" keeps butterflies and bees happy from spring through fall. Over the summer, the flowers age to brown, and then the chocolate-colored seed heads attract finches and other seed-eating birds. As the plant ages and grows taller, the lower branches can be trimmed up to extenuate the shaggy bark. The plant can also be kept dense and to size by winter pruning before spring growth, when flower buds develop. The plant readily self-seeds in garden settings.

Highly attractive to bees and butterflies, especially hairstreaks and blues; birds eat the seeds; larval host for up to 23 butterfly species.

Silver Bush Lupine

Scientific Name *Lupinus albifrons*

Family Legume (Fabaceae)

Plant Characteristics Mounding, spreading evergreen shrub with trunk or multiple stems 3–5 feet tall and wide; densely foliated, with silvery-hairy leaves that have fingerlike lobes; blue-violet flowers on dense, erect spikes. Deer resistant.

USDA Hardiness Zones 8a–10a

Bloom Period Spring–summer (March–July)

Growing Conditions Full sun; coarse, well-draining soils; water 1x/month once established.

A bushy, waist-high, silvery lupine covered with a wave of 6- to 12-inch spikes of brilliant violet flowers will be the top attraction in your garden, especially for bumblebees, the chief pollinator, and butterflies, which sip the nectar. Silvery hairs cover the stems and leaves, making this "ever-gray" plant a year-round foliage accent for sunny garden backgrounds, garden walls, mixed borders, courtyards, or poolside container plantings. Four varieties occur in the state, each with slightly different habitat needs. The bushy variety, *albifrons*, is the most widespread, but other varieties and selections are prostrate wildflowers. As a low-growing, spreading ground cover, the dwarf variety, *collinus*, is only 8–18 inches tall and wide. Grape Soda Lupine (*L. excubitus*) is indistinguishable from Silver Bush Lupine in both the field and yard.

Attracts bumblebees and butterflies; larval host for up to 58 species of butterflies and moths.

St. Catherine's Lace

Scientific Name *Eriogonum giganteum*

Family Buckwheat (Polygonaceae)

Plant Characteristics Rounded, evergreen shrub with multiple branches, 3–8 feet tall and wide; leaves oval, silvery gray, woolly to hairy; flowers small, creamy to pinkish, in 12-inch-wide, flat-topped clusters on stems above foliage; spent flowers rusty red. Deer resistant.

USDA Hardiness Zones 8b–10b

Bloom Period Spring–summer (March–August)

Growing Conditions Full sun (coastal), partial sun (inland); sandy, clayey, well-draining soils; water 1x/month in summer once established.

Designated an "All-Star" California landscape plant by the UC Davis Arboretum, this native of the Channel Islands thrives in mainland pollinator gardens. As a year-round keystone plant, it provides butterflies and bees with huge clusters of nectar-rich flowers, abundant seeds for resident and migrating birds, and ample cover and shade for birds and other animals. Its large size makes it suitable as a background, mixed border, or screen planting, or as a stand-alone focal point. It partners well with Hollyleaf Cherry, 'Canyon Silver' Catalina Silver-Lace, sumacs, and Bush Monkeyflower; it also grows rapidly and self-seeds. Manage size by lightly trimming in early spring before buds form. Extra summer water keeps it lush. It hybridizes with California Buckwheat, so naturalized populations could compromise the native species' gene pool.

Highly attractive to butterflies, bees, and other pollinators; provides cover and seeds for birds; larval host for up to 12 butterflies and moths, including the Avalon Scrub-Hairstreak (Strymon avalona).

Toyon

Scientific Name *Heteromeles arbutifolia*

Family Rose (Rosaceae)

Plant Characteristics Evergreen shrub 6–8 feet tall to small tree 12–20 feet tall; leaves dark green, elliptical, 2–4 inches long; clusters of creamy flowers develop into red berries. New growth palatable to deer.

USDA Hardiness Zones 7a–10b

Bloom Period Summer (June–August); fruit: fall–winter

Growing Conditions Full sun, partial shade; well-draining soils; water 1x/month until established; no summer water.

Native to chaparral from Eureka to San Diego, this widespread, wildlife-friendly evergreen is a valued all-season addition to habitat gardens. It provides clusters of nectar-rich summer flowers for butterflies and bees, along with colorful bundles of red fruit for birds in the winter, as well as nesting and cover in the dense evergreen foliage. Found on many top-10 landscape lists, Toyon can be a floral and foliage accent against a wall or walkway; an anchor for a landscape oval; a screen or border; or a mixed hedge with California Coffeeberry, Island Bush Poppy, or manzanita or ceanothus species. Whether a mounding shrub or trimmed up into an ornate, multi-trunked tree, Toyon is a wildlife-garden standout. Do any structural pruning and shaping after the fruit fades, as it flowers on new growth. The 'Davis Gold' cultivar has yellow berries.

Attracts butterflies and bees; provides nesting, shelter, and winter food for birds; larval host for Pacific Azure Butterfly (Celastrina echo) and up to 6 moth species.

Twinberry Honeysuckle

Scientific Name *Lonicera involucrata* var. *ledebourii*

Family Honeysuckle (Caprifoliaceae)

Plant Characteristics Deciduous, bushy shrub 3–9 feet tall, 4–5 feet wide; bright-green leaves elliptical, 2–5 inches long; flowers paired, tubular, orange-tinged yellow, ¾ inch long; fruit a ⅓-inch berry. Deer resistant.

USDA Hardiness Zones 6a–10b

Bloom Period Spring–summer (April–July)

Growing Conditions Full sun, partial shade; moist, sandy, loamy, well-draining soils; water 1x/week in summer once established.

Occurring in open edge habitats, in periodically damp soils, this densely foliated shrub will be happy in a similar garden habitat, and so will the birds and insect pollinators. In the spring, the paired, tubular flowers attract hummingbirds, butterflies, bees; then, in the summer, birds devour the juicy fruit. This underrated ornamental adds bright-green foliage color and cover for birds, and by late summer, the leaflike bracts around the blue-black berries turn a dark red for a striking green-red-black color contrast. Use as a garden background, wall border, summer screen, slope planting, or ornamental specimen. It pairs well with Pacific Ninebark, Cream Bush, currants, and Red Osier Dogwood. The inland *involucrata* variety, widespread in the West, has solid-yellow flowers and similar habitat requirements.

Attracts hummingbirds, butterflies, bees, and many other insects; provides food and cover for birds; larval host for Chalcedon Checkerspot (Euphydryas chalcedona) *and up to 25 other butterfly and moth species.*

Western Azalea

Scientific Name *Rhododendron occidentale*

Family Heath (Ericaceae)

Plant Characteristics Deciduous, erect to spreading, multistemmed shrub 4–12 feet tall and wide; leaves elliptical, 1–4 inches long, orange in fall; flowers 1–2 inches wide in clusters of 3–15 on branch ends, fragrant, white (usually) to pink, with a yellow splotch on upper petal. Deer resistant.

USDA Hardiness Zones 6a–10b

Bloom Period Spring–summer (May–June)

Growing Conditions Performs best in partial shade, tolerates full sun in protected settings; moist, rich, acidic, well-draining soils; water 1x/week in summer once established.

This popular azalea is native to forests from Monterey northward on moist, wooded slopes; in canyons; and at stream and pond edges. It prefers serpentine soils with high organic content, moist (but not water-logged) roots, and enough sun to produce showy, perfumed flowers, but not so much sun that its growth is stunted. It needs circulating air to prevent leaf mildew, so don't hem it in with a crowded mixed planting. Mulch the roots to keep them cool. You'll thrill at the colorful spectacle when flamboyant flowers cover the shrub, and again in fall when the leaves turn golden yellow. If you can't replicate its forest habitat, put one in a pot on a drip line on your patio. Flower color varies in nature from white to rosy pink, allowing for a number of cultivars and hybrids. The other native azalea, California Rosebay (*R. macrophyllum*), evergreen with rosy-purple flowers, has similar garden requirements.

Attracts butterflies, bees, hummingbirds, and other pollinators; provides cover for birds; larval host for comma butterflies (Polygonia spp.), Gray Hairstreaks (Strymon melinus), and up to 21 other butterfly and moth species.

Western Mock Orange

Scientific Name *Philadelphus lewisii*

Family Hydrangea (Hydrangeaceae)

Plant Characteristics Deciduous shrub with erect, vaselike, arching branches 6–9 feet tall and 4–6 feet wide; leaves oval, up to 3 inches long, yellow in fall; flowers white, fragrant, 2 inches wide; fruit a small capsule. Deer resistant.

USDA Hardiness Zones 5a–10b

Bloom Period Spring–summer (May–June)

Growing Conditions Full sun, partial shade; adaptable, moist to dry, well-draining soils; water 3x/month in summer.

Native to moist canyons and dry slopes in Northern California forests and foothill chaparral of the Eastern Sierras, this garden-friendly shrub is adapted to open sun, understory shade, and moist or dry conditions. Prized for its masses of showy, white flowers that blanket the tree in the spring, Western Mock Orange floods your garden with a sweet, citrusy aroma—an irresistible invitation for bees and butterflies. Use it in hedges and privacy screens, as a background garden anchor, and as a specimen accent planting. It partners well with Western Redbud, Western Spice Bush, California Coffeeberry, and ceanothus selections. Regular light pruning maintains the structure and density, and in hot, sunny settings, extra water improves blooming.

Attracts bees, butterflies, and other small pollinators; provides shelter and seeds for birds.

Western Spice Bush

Scientific Name *Calycanthus occidentalis*

Family Sweetshrub (Calycanthaceae)

Plant Characteristics Deciduous, rounded, multi stemmed, thicket-forming shrub 4–12 feet tall and wide; leaves 3–8 inches long, elliptical, leathery, aromatic; flower 2–3 inches wide, dark red; fruit a 2-inch-long capsule. Deer resistant.

USDA Hardiness Zones 7a–10b

Bloom Period Spring–summer (April–August)

Growing Conditions Performs best in partial shade, tolerates full sun with extra water; moist, well-draining, sandy, loamy, clayey soils; water 1–2x/month in summer.

Native to moist, shady places; canyons; and streambanks, this aromatic shrub with dense, bright-green foliage provides good shelter for birds and is pollinated by sap beetles. It suckers to form thickets, ideal for border and privacy hedges and background or screen plantings against a wall or fence. Prune it as a specimen shrub or into a small, multistemmed accent tree covered with showy flowers. In the fall, the yellow leaves and persistent woody seed capsules add extra color. It may need root sprouts removed. To shape and maintain compactness, prune immediately after flowering, and severely every 3–4 years. In inland sites, it will burn in hot sun or without sufficient irrigation.

Attracts butterflies, bees, beetles, and other pollinators; provides shelter for birds; larval host for moths.

Western Spirea

Scientific Name *Spiraea douglasii*

Family Rose (Rosaceae)

Plant Characteristics Deciduous, clump-forming, rhizomatous shrub; multiple stems 3–6 feet tall and wide; leaves oval, 1–4 inches long, yellow in fall; small, pink flowers in dense, pyramidal clusters 3–8 inches long. Deer resistant.

USDA Hardiness Zones 5a–10b

Bloom Period Summer (July–August)

Growing Conditions Partial shade, full sun; moist, sandy, loamy, fast- to slow-draining soils; requires regular moisture.

Native to riparian areas, wet meadows, and open edges in conifer forests, this attractive shrub requires regular moisture and is suitable for woodland gardens in the Coast Ranges and northward. In late summer, showy clusters of rosy flowers create a wave of color and a nectar-rich food source for pollinators. It's a showstopper as a background hedge or border, and it's a good companion for other woodland plants, such as Red Osier Dogwood, Western Azalea, and Chokecherry (all deciduous). For four-season foliage, pair with evergreens like Toyon, Bush Anemone, and California Coffeeberry. It spreads by rhizomes and will naturalize in moist wildscape areas. A number of garden-friendly hybrids have been developed with this species. Mountain Spirea (*S. splendens*), a similar species with flat-topped flower clusters, is native at 2,000–11,000 feet. Japanese selections and cultivars are available but not recommended for native plant gardens.

Attracts hummingbirds, butterflies, bees, and other pollinators; provides cover for birds; larval host for Lorquin's Admiral (Limenitis lorquini) and up to 33 other butterfly and moth species.

Woolly Blue Curls

Scientific Name *Trichostema lanatum*

Family Mint (Lamiaceae)

Plant Characteristics Evergreen, erect, multibranched shrub 3–5 feet tall and wide; leaves narrow, shiny above, woolly below; flowers blue to lavender and pink, tubular with arching lips, in dense, hairy whorls along stems. Deer resistant.

USDA Hardiness Zones 7a–10b

Bloom Period Spring–summer (March–August)

Growing Conditions Full sun, partial shade; well-draining soils; water in summer until established, then lightly 1x/month.

With its attractive foliage; showy, long-blooming flowers; and a medium-size, vaselike shape, this eye-catching top-10 selection will delight gardeners and pollinators alike. The vibrant plant makes a dramatic midgarden or background color accent; highlights a pollinator-habitat island; and brightens borders, walls, and view gardens. For colorscaping and increased pollinator diversity, partner with Hummingbird Trumpet, buckwheats, currants and gooseberries, goldenrod species, or Bush Monkeyflower. Be sure to choose a well-draining site for this drought-tolerant chaparral native. Sustained or regular moisture is the kiss of death. Several cultivars, especially 'Cuesta Ridge,' are particularly garden hardy.

Attracts hummingbirds, butterflies, bees, and other pollinators; larval host for up to 5 species of butterflies and moths.

Yankee Point Ceanothus

Scientific Name *Ceanothus griseus* 'Yankee Point'

Family Buckthorn (Rhamnaceae)

Plant Characteristics Low-growing evergreen 2–3 feet tall to 12 feet wide, with sprawling to mounding branches; dark-green, elliptical leaves; flower clusters dark blue. Palatable to deer.

USDA Hardiness Zones 8a–10b

Bloom Period Winter–spring (February–June)

Growing Conditions Full sun (coastal), afternoon shade (inland); sandy, clayey, well-draining soils; inland, water 1–2x/month in summer.

Widespread and commonly used as a ground cover, this coastal native does well inland if given afternoon shade and extra water, especially in the summer. The sprawling branches are perfect as a fill-in ground cover, border, accent over a raised-garden wall or boulder, or (if allowed to build up) a trimmed hedge. Prune after flowering to maintain the desired shape. For a dramatic colorscape, mix with Hummingbird Sage (red), Hummingbird Trumpet (red), or California Buckwheat (white). The abundant flowers provide an early source of nectar for butterflies and hummingbirds. Also named *Ceanothus thyrsiflorus* var. *griseus* 'Yankee Point.'

Attracts hummingbirds, butterflies, and other pollinators; provides nesting and cover for birds; larval host for Spring Azure, Echo Blue, Pacuvius Duskywing, California Tortoiseshell, Pale Swallowtail, and Hedgerow Hairstreak Butterflies.

Leopard Lily

Meadowfoam

Sacred Datura

Wildflowers

Checker Bloom

Seaside Daisy

Baby Blue Eyes

Yarrow

Choosing wildflowers for your pollinator garden is where you can let your imagination and creativity run wild. Their beauty will bring joy with every bud that pops open and every butterfly and bee that dives in for a sip of nectar. Select perennials for dependable year-after-year blooms, but don't neglect the ephemeral beauty of annuals. Coordinate bloom times for mass or fill-in plantings and color and size combinations. Your goal is a long-blooming selection that will attract a diversity of pollinators.

Indian Pink

Showy Milkweed

California Golden Violet

Baby Blue Eyes

Scientific Name *Nemophila menziesii*

Family Waterleaf (Hydrophyllaceae)

Plant Characteristics Annual with many delicate, spreading stems 4–10 inches tall; leaves compound, 2 inches long, with 5–13 rounded segments; flowers cup shaped, 1–2 inches wide, pale blue with a white center, often with lines. Palatable to deer.

USDA Hardiness Zones 7b–11a

Bloom Period Winter–summer (February–June)

Growing Conditions Full sun, partial shade; sandy, loamy, well-draining soils; water 2x/month in winter/spring if rains fail.

Native to openings in coastal scrub, chaparral, valley grasslands, and woodlands, this perky, pretty little annual makes an eye-catching accent when mass-planted or mixed with California Poppies, Tidy Tips, California Goldfields, or any of California's other gorgeous annual wildflowers. Use as a stunning color fill-in for sunny, open spots; slopes; and raised beds. Plant as accents around boulders or along walkways, or in pool or patio gardens. It's beautiful trailing over baskets and containers. Sow seeds or wildflower annual mixes in the fall before frost, and wait for the spring explosion of color. Over time a seed bank will build in the soil—proving that nature lets no ground go uncovered.

Attracts butterflies, bees, and other pollinators; larval host for Funereal Duskywing Butterfly (Erynnis funeralis) and up to 4 moth species.

Blue-Eyed Grass

Scientific Name *Sisyrinchium bellum*

Family Iris (Iridaceae)

Plant Characteristics Clumping, summer-dormant perennial with many stems, 1–2 feet tall and wide; leaf blades narrow, grasslike, mostly basal from rhizome nodes; flowers purplish blue with yellow throats, 1 inch wide. Deer resistant.

USDA Hardiness Zones 7a–10b

Bloom Period Spring (March–May)

Growing Conditions Full sun, partial shade; sandy to clayey, well-draining soils; water 2x/month in summer once established.

Native to meadows and grasslands from coast to mountains, this top-rated garden flower is pollinated by native bees, hover flies (bee mimics), and beetles, all major players in a pollinator habitat. Blue-Eyed Grass adds a splash of color to a mixed border, walkway, garden foreground, sunny slope, or container planting. Its vibrant flowers and dense mounds of basal leaves soften hardscape boulders and retaining walls. The hues of its deep-blue-to-purple flowers blend well with Coyote Mint, Seaside Daisy, and Yarrow, and they add flower and foliage color when nestled with Giant Rye Grass and other bunchgrasses. Extra water will keep Blue-Eyed Grass flush until it dies to the ground in the summer heat. This jewel readily self-sows, or you can divide the rhizomes, so that it will brighten your garden spring after spring. Cultivars with white or various shades of blue flowers are available, along with yellow Golden-Eyed Grass (*S. californicum*).

Attracts butterflies, bees, and other small pollinators.

Broadleaf Lupine

Scientific Name *Lupinus latifolius*

Family Legume (Fabaceae)

Plant Characteristics Erect, herbaceous perennial with leafy, branching stems 1–4 feet tall; leaves palmate with 5–11 fingerlike leaflets 1–3 inches long; flowers fragrant, purple to blue, pealike, 1–2 inches long, in dense whorls on 1-foot-long spikes. Deer resistant.

USDA Hardiness Zones 5b–10b

Bloom Period Spring–summer (April–July)

Growing Conditions Full sun, partial shade; moist, coarse, well-draining soils; water 2x/month in summer.

Common in periodically moist, shady to open woodlands and meadows, this clump-forming perennial spreads by rhizomes and seeds to form lush colonies of nectar-rich flowers. Replicate its habitat in your garden, and you'll have a five-star pollinator attraction. It blooms from the bottom of the spike upward, and, when pollinated, the white upper banner petal turns reddish, like a traffic light, to direct the bees to fresh blooms. For dramatic effect, mass-plant Broadleaf Lupine in borders, backgrounds, open slopes, or a habitat island. For added color and habitat richness, mix with Foothill Penstemon, Checker Bloom, or buckwheats. It dies to the ground in winter, but delay cleanup until the pods split open and release the seeds.

Attracts bees, butterflies, and many other pollinators; larval host for Painted Lady (Vanessa cardui), Gray Hairstreak (Strymon melinus), Acmon Blue (Plebejus acmon), and up to 52 other butterfly and moth species.

California Bee Plant

Scientific Name *Scrophularia californica*

Family Figwort (Scrophulariaceae)

Plant Characteristics Herbaceous perennial with slender stem 3–5 feet tall; leaves triangular with serrated edges; flowers small, red, pouchlike, ½ inch long, with open, spikelike clusters spreading along upper stem; fruit a small, seed-filled capsule. Deer resistant.

USDA Hardiness Zones 7a–10b

Bloom Period Spring–summer (April–July)

Growing Conditions Full sun (coastal), partial shade (inland); sandy, loamy, heavy, clayey, well-draining soils; water 1x/month in summer once established.

Like chocolate kisses, delicious treats sometimes come in small packages. Though thumbnail-size, the understated maroon flowers pack a nectar-rich prize for hummingbirds, bumblebees, and other pollinators. One tall, gangly stem can have dozens of tiny flowers, and a mob of pollinators large and small. Birds move in as soon as the seeds ripen. Best suited to an informal wildscape cluster, naturalized corner, or slope or meadow mixed planting, California Bee Plant makes a well-rounded habitat partner with Narrowleaf Milkweed, Western Red Columbine, Hooker's Evening Primrose, and Common Sunflower. Native to chaparral, meadows, open woodlands, and moist places, it appreciates partial shade and extra summer water in hot inland gardens.

Attracts hummingbirds, bees, butterflies, and other pollinators; birds eat the seeds; larval host for Chalcedon Checkerspot (Euphydryas chalcedona), Common Buckeye (Junonia coenia), and up to 12 other butterfly and moth species.

California Goldenrod

Scientific Name *Solidago velutina* ssp. *californica*

Family Aster (Asteraceae)

Plant Characteristics Leafy, hairy, herbaceous perennial with stems 1–5 feet tall; leaves narrow, pointed, 2–5 inches long; flower heads small, yellow, in dense clusters. Deer resistant.

USDA Hardiness Zones 6a–10b

Bloom Period Summer–fall (July–October)

Growing Conditions Full sun, partial shade; coarse, well-draining soils; water 1–2x/month once established.

With multiple shoulder-high stems topped with dense, pyramidal to wandlike clusters, each with up to 100 small flowers, these pollen powerhouses are one of the most important sources of fall pollinator food, especially for honeybees and migrating Monarch Butterflies. The Xerces Society lists goldenrods—with nectar that is 33% sugar—in its book *Top 100 Plants to Feed the Bees*. In your garden, use them for backgrounds, walkway borders, color patches, or wall accents. Partner with buckwheats, milkweeds, Red Osier Dogwood, and other spring and summer bloomers for extended pollinator resources. Numerous species and cultivars exist, from 1 to 5 feet tall, so choose one that matches your design. Extra water promotes vigorous growth, but goldenrods spread by rhizomes and can become aggressive in garden soils. Also called Velvet or Three-Nerved Goldenrod.

Highly attractive to all insect pollinators; larval host for up to 39 butterfly and moth species.

California Golden Violet

Scientific Name *Viola pedunculata*

Family Violet (Violaceae)

Plant Characteristics Clumping, herbaceous perennial with multiple leafy, erect to trailing stems 2–15 inches tall; leaves heart shaped on 1- to 3-inch-long stalks; flowers 1½ inches wide with 5 spreading, yellow petals; lower 3 petals have dark nectar guide lines leading into the throat. Deer resistant.

USDA Hardiness Zones 8b–11a

Bloom Period Winter–spring (February–April)

Growing Conditions Prefers partial shade, tolerates full sun; rich, well-draining soils; extra water in summer inland, none coastal.

This cheerful little flower naturally grows on moist, grassy slopes in coastal scrub and prairies, foothills, and oak woodlands. It thrives in garden soils in partial shade and spreads by rhizomes to form a dense ground cover or border, and it adds a floral/foliage highlight to a foreground or mixed planting. In the Bay Area, this violet is the only host plant for the critically endangered Callippe Silverspot Butterfly (*Speyeria callippe callippe*). Fritillaries lay their eggs in leaf litter near violets; the eggs hatch and overwinter in the litter, and the caterpillars then feed on the new violet leaves in the spring—so keep your habitat a little wild and the leaf litter unkempt. Besides depending on insect pollinators, violets produce tiny, petal-less flowers on the stem that self-pollinate and set copious seeds.

Attracts butterflies, bees, and other native pollinators; larval host for the endangered Callippe Silverspot (Speyeria callippe callippe) and Myrtle's and Behren's Silverspots (Speyeria zerene spp.), along with up to 20 additional butterfly species.

California Goldfields

Scientific Name *Lasthenia californica*

Family Aster (Asteraceae)

Plant Characteristics Annual wildflower with erect stems up to 16 inches tall; leaves linear to oblong, 1½ inches long; flower head 1 inch wide, with 6–13 yellow rays and yellow disk. Deer resistant.

USDA Hardiness Zones 7a–10b

Bloom Period Spring (March–May)

Growing Conditions Full sun; a variety of well-draining soils; needs winter rain.

Spring-blooming annuals bring a special delight to a garden when they burst into bloom with splashes of vivid color. The brilliant yellows, reds, oranges, and blues serve one purpose for the flowers: to attract as many pollinators as possible. One way to get a bee or butterfly's attention is through synchronized mass-blooming. In your garden, annuals will paint sunny wildscape areas, foregrounds, borders, and slopes with multicolored hues. Goldfields makes up for its small size with a multitude of yellow blooms that blend beautifully with Globe Gilia, Baby Blue Eyes, Tidy Tips, and California Poppies. California has 16 *Lasthenia* species, all very similar and popular in wildflower seed mixes. Sow the seeds in winter; they germinate easily and self-sow. As the seed bank builds in your habitat landscape, you'll have years of nectar-rich super-blooms. Extra water in dry years increases germination and blooming.

Pollinated by bees; attracts butterflies and other pollinators.

California Poppy

Scientific Name *Eschscholzia californica*

Family Poppy (Papaveraceae)

Plant Characteristics Annual or perennial (in frost-free regions), clumping wildflower with multiple stems up to 18 inches tall and wide; leaves blue-green, with feathery lobes; flowers yellow to orange, 2–3 inches wide. Deer resistant.

USDA Hardiness Zones 8a–10b

Bloom Period Winter–summer (February–June)

Growing Conditions Full sun and coarse, well-draining soils.

Germinated by winter rains, these spectacular flowers often carpet rocky slopes and fields with flamboyant color. In your garden, they will reseed and provide gorgeous patches spring after spring. Plant along walkways or patios; as garden fill-ins; or as wall, boulder, or cacti accents. To create a super-bloom that gets more glamorous as the soil's seed bank builds over time, mix with Globe Gilia, Baby Blue Eyes, and Tidy Tips. Extend the color season and pollinator diversity by mixing with perennials such as Canyon (Red) Larkspur, Blue-Eyed Grass, and Coyote Mint. Sow seeds directly onto coarse soils in the winter, or start in pots. Numerous cultivars and color varieties are available, but honestly, the true species needs no improvement.

Attracts butterflies, bees, and other pollinators; birds eat the seeds; larval host for up to 7 butterfly and moth species.

Canyon (Red) Larkspur

Scientific Name *Delphinium nudicaule*

Family Buttercup (Ranunculaceae)

Plant Characteristics Herbaceous perennial with slender, branching stems 6–20 inches tall; leaves rounded, with deep, narrow lobes; scarlet flowers tubular, ½ inch wide, with symmetrical, petal-like lobes and a rear spur, occurring in loose spikes. All parts toxic. Deer resistant.

USDA Hardiness Zones 7a–11a

Bloom Period Spring–summer (March–July)

Growing Conditions Partial shade; coarse, rocky, well-draining soils; water 1–2x/month in spring to encourage blooming.

Mass-plant these knee-high natives with flamboyant spikes of scarlet flowers, and behold the hummingbird circus. The flowers have stout, 1-inch-long spurs that hold the nectary glands. Plant a patch of color in a garden foreground, along a border, or in a container. 'Redcap' is a compact selection with orange-red flowers. For extended color-scaping and habitat diversity, plant with shade-tolerant Western Red Columbine, Chinese Houses, and Yarrow. Native to streambanks and spring seeps in partial shade, emerging sprouts appreciate extra spring water in dry years. No summer water is needed because the deep-rooted perennials die back by late summer; larkspurs self-sow and naturalize. Northern California has more than a dozen larkspur species—mostly blue and white, with unequal lobes designed for bumblebee pollination. Some species are common in seed mixes; all have similar garden uses.

Attracts hummingbirds, bumblebees, and other pollinators; larval host for up to 3 moth species.

171

Checker Bloom

Scientific Name *Sidalcea malviflora*

Family Mallow (Malvaceae)

Plant Characteristics Herbaceous perennial with multiple 2- to 4-foot-tall, branching stems from base; leaves rounded, lobed; flowers pink to red, cup shaped, 1 inch wide, in spikes along stems. Deer resistant.

USDA Hardiness Zones 6a–10a

Bloom Period Spring–summer (May–August)

Growing Conditions Full sun, partial shade; fertile, loamy, well-draining soils; water 1x/month once established.

Native from coastal sage scrub to chaparral, inland grasslands, and open woodlands from San Diego to Oregon, this plant takes off in a garden setting. Dense clusters of erect, waist-high stems covered with flamboyant, bright-pink, hollyhock-like blooms scream for the attention of butterflies, as well as bees and hummingbirds. Use as a stunning vertical background or midgarden accent, or in a mixed walkway border with Blue-Eyed Grass, Tansy-Leaf Phacelia, Yarrow, larkspurs, penstemons, or Leopard Lily. Cut back spent stems after seeds disperse. Easily propagated; sow in spring after danger of frost, pack seeds into soil, or use starter pots. Also called Checker Mallow.

Attracts butterflies, bees, and hummingbirds; larval host for West Coast Lady (Vanessa annabella), Gray Hairstreak (Strymon melinus), and skipper butterflies (Pyrgus spp.).

Chinese Houses

Scientific Name *Collinsia heterophylla*

Family Plantain (Plantaginaceae)

Plant Characteristics Upright annual with stems 4–24 inches tall; leaves opposite, slender; flowers pealike, with lilac to white upper lip and purple lower lip; blooms are whorled around stem in separated clusters. Deer resistant.

USDA Hardiness Zones 7a–10b

Bloom Period Winter–spring (February–April)

Growing Conditions Partial shade; sandy, loamy, well-draining soils; water 2x/month in spring to encourage blooming.

Unlike most sun-loving annuals, this widespread native from chaparral and coastal sage scrub to oak woodlands prefers partial to bright shade. The waving stems, topped with 1-foot-long spikes of stunning flowers, create a pollinator picnic that lasts for up to a month. But not everyone is welcome. The flower's lower-petal "landing pad" for bees is levered to open only for those bees that are large enough for efficient pollination. If the bee is heavy enough, the petal pops open to reveal the pollen and nectar hidden in the throat. Use Chinese Houses as an understory cover, fill-in, and spot color accent. For a spring colorscape that keeps bees and butterflies working overtime, mass-plant with Tidy Tips, Globe Gilia, Blue-Eyed Grass, and *Clarkia* species. Sow seeds in the autumn. The flower readily naturalizes and self-seeds to establish a seed bank that keeps giving for years.

Attracts bees and butterflies; larval host plant for Variable and Edith Checkerspot Butterflies (Euphydryas spp.).

Coast Aster

Scientific Name *Symphyotrichum chilense*

Family Aster (Asteraceae)

Plant Characteristics Erect, herbaceous perennial with several branching stems 1–3 feet tall; leaves slender, 1–4 inches long; flower head 1½–2 inches wide; rays blue, violet, pink, or whitish; disk yellow; clusters are open-branched on stems. Deer resistant.

USDA Hardiness Zones 6a–10b

Bloom Period Summer–fall (June–October)

Growing Conditions Full sun, partial shade; coarse, well-draining soils; water 1–2x/month in summer once established.

Native to chaparral, grasslands, and disturbed areas from the coast to the foothills, this gangly pollinator favorite feels right at home in a garden setting. By summer, clusters of perky, lavender to whitish-pink, daisylike flowers cover the waist-high stems. One of UC Davis's top 10 plants for bees, asters are an important summer–fall food source for migrating Monarch Butterflies and nesting bees. Best suited for wildscapes, meadow plantings, or mixed backgrounds, it complements goldenrod species, Hummingbird Trumpet, Common Sunflower, and Canyon Prince Wild Rye Grass. Dwarf cultivars, suitable as ground covers and foregrounds, are available. Coast Aster readily self-sows with fluffy, wind-blown seeds and spreads by rhizomes; thus, it can become invasive. Cut the dead stems to the ground in the winter. Also called Pacific or California Aster.

Attracts butterflies, bees, and other pollinators; birds eat the seeds; larval host for Painted Lady (Vanessa cardui) and Crescent (Chlosyne spp.) butterflies and up to 9 moth species.

Coast Buckwheat

Scientific Name *Eriogonum latifolium*

Family Buckwheat (Polygonaceae)

Plant Characteristics Evergreen, mat-forming sub-shrub or perennial has thick rosette of oval leaves with cob-webby hair; dense, spherical clusters of small, white-to-pink flowers bloom on 1-inch-tall stems. Deer resistant but rabbit palatable.

USDA Hardiness Zones 8a–11a

Bloom Period Summer–fall (July–September)

Growing Conditions Full sun (coastal); partial shade (inland); sandy, well-draining soils; water 1x/month in summer if outside its natural range.

Native to coastal scrub, flats, mesas, and grasslands, this ground cover thrives with cool summers, regular moisture, and sandy soils. Dozens of 1-foot-tall stems, topped with golf ball–size, white-to-pink flower clusters, punctuate the 1–2 foot broad rosettes of gray-green leaves. Bees and butterflies feast on the nectar-rich flowers, which fade to rusty red. Use this mounding ground cover as a walkway border or boulder accent, to drape a raised garden wall, or in a mixed planting with Seaside Daisy, Yellow Sand-Verbena, Coyote Mint, or Spreading Coastal Gumplant. Coast Buckwheat is stress deciduous, so if you plant it outside of its coastal range, give it extra summer water to keep it robust. The Xerces Society considers buckwheat species must-have plants for California habitat gardens.

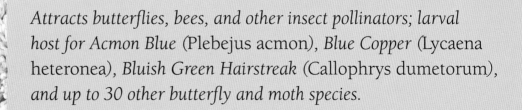

Attracts butterflies, bees, and other insect pollinators; larval host for Acmon Blue (Plebejus acmon), Blue Copper (Lycaena heteronea), Bluish Green Hairstreak (Callophrys dumetorum), and up to 30 other butterfly and moth species.

Common Madia

Scientific Name *Madia elegans*

Family Aster (Asteraceae)

Plant Characteristics Upright annual with 1- to 4-foot-tall stem topped with a dense, 3-foot-wide array of lateral branches; leaves narrow to lance shaped, 1–8 inches long; flower head 1–2 inches wide with 5–22 rays, pure yellow or with a red base, disk yellow. Deer resistant.

USDA Hardiness Zones All zones

Bloom Period Summer–fall (June–November)

Growing Conditions Full sun; coarse to clayey soils; no extra water needed if winter rains are sufficient.

Also called Showy Tarweed, this widespread species occurs in grasslands, shrublands, meadows, and disturbed areas, so it thrives in a garden setting. Unlike most annuals, it doesn't get started until midsummer, when pollinators need pollen and nectar the most; then it goes gangbusters. Scores of showy flowers cover the widely branching, waist-high stems. Bees are most active in the morning, so that's when the flowers open. They close by midday, when the bees take a siesta; then they often open again in the cool of a summer evening. Madia is flamboyant, with showy flowers, but it's a little rambunctious for formal gardens. Use it in a background wildscape, wall border, or meadow planting. Goldfinches adore the small, sunflower-like seeds. Sow in fall, then let it self-sow and build a seed bank in the soil for years of encore performances.

Highly attractive to bees, along with butterflies and many other insects; birds eat the seeds; larval host for 3 moth species.

Common Sunflower

Scientific Name *Helianthus annuus*

Family Aster (Asteraceae)

Plant Characteristics Annual with stout, branching stem 3–10 feet tall; leaves large, rough, heart shaped; flower head 3–6 inches wide, with yellow rays and brown disk. Deer resistant.

USDA Hardiness Zones 2a–11a

Bloom Period Summer (June–August)

Growing Conditions Full sun; coarse, well-draining soils; water 1x/month.

If the birds and the bees formed a committee, they might vote the Common Sunflower their favorite flower. One massive plant can have 25–75 blooms, each packed with nectar and pollen. Goldfinches and other seed-eating birds feast on the dried flower heads. Dozens of cultivars exist in shades of red and orange, from 2-foot dwarfs to 15-foot giants with 12-inch flower heads. So, really, find a place for this pollinator self-sustaining ecosystem "supermarket." Plant a wildscape "forest" of 5–10 along a back wall or neglected space, or place 1–2 as a garden background accent. Multicolored dwarf cultivars make an attractive border, window planter, or patio container planting. More sun and water make bigger plants. Sunflowers famously self-sow, but they are easy to control in a garden. Not all sunflower cultivar seeds are equal as food for birds, so it's best to choose the local native species or similar.

Attracts bees, butterflies, and other pollinators; birds eat the seeds and leaves; larval host for up to 37 butterflies and moths.

Common Woolly Sunflower

Scientific Name *Eriophyllum lanatum*

Family Aster (Asteraceae)

Plant Characteristics Clump-forming, herbaceous perennial with multiple stems 4–24 inches tall; ornate grayish leaves lance shaped, up to 3 inches long, hairy to woolly; flower heads 1–2 inches wide on 1- to 12-inch-tall stalks, with 5–13 yellow ray flowers and a yellow disk. Deer resistant.

USDA Hardiness Zones 5b–10b

Bloom Period Spring–summer (May–August)

Growing Conditions Full sun, partial shade; dry, sandy, rocky, well-draining soils; water 1–2x/month in summer once established.

Also called Oregon Sunshine, this widespread native grows from sagebrush scrub and valley grasslands to foothill woodlands and conifer forests of the northern and Sierra ranges. With 10 varieties and natural hybrids, the plant has yielded many horticultural selections, from matlike to 2 feet tall and with different habitat needs. But regardless of cultivar, bees and butterflies mob the clusters of daisylike flowers. For habitat diversity and colorscaping, the perky yellow flowers and gray-green leaves partner well with Coast (white) and Sulphur (yellow) Buckwheats, Yarrow (white/yellow), Foothill Penstemon (blue), and Coyote Mint (pink). Use it as a garden foreground, as a fill-in color accent, and in small habitat islands.

Attracts bees, butterflies, and many other insect pollinators; larval host for up to 7 moth species.

Coyote Mint

Scientific Name *Monardella villosa*

Family Mint (Lamiaceae)

Plant Characteristics Low-growing to mounding evergreen 1–2 feet tall by 3 feet wide, with multiple branches from base; leaves triangular–oval, narrow, gray-green, 1¼ inches long; flowers tubular, pink to lavender, in dense clusters 1½ inches wide. Deer resistant.

USDA Hardiness Zones 8b–10b

Bloom Period Summer (June–August)

Growing Conditions Full sun, partial shade; sandy, gravelly, well-draining soils; water 1x/month in summer once established.

Native to chaparral and coastal sage scrub, this low-mounding evergreen is a versatile addition to pollinator gardens. Dense clusters of small, fragrant, pom-pom-like flowers cover the slender, spreading stems. Use it as a fill-in ground cover; as a foreground accent with medium-size shrubs; in a mixed border with Sulphur Buckwheat, Seaside Daisy, or other low-growing plants; along a walkway; or as a container plant. Its summer flowers add color after spring bloomers fade, and they provide a rich nectar source loved by butterflies. It's drought tolerant with a deep taproot, but extra summer water and afternoon shade will extend blooming. Trim back in the winter to encourage dense foliage.

Highly attractive to butterflies, bees, hummingbirds, and other pollinators; larval host for up to 8 moth species.

Douglas Iris

Scientific Name *Iris douglasiana*

Family Iris (Iridaceae)

Plant Characteristics Evergreen that forms dense, leafy clumps 1–3 feet tall and 2–4 feet wide from spreading rhizomes; leaf blades swordlike, 1–3 feet long; typical iris flowers top 1- to 2-foot-tall stems; petals lavender, purple, blue, or cream, lined with gold and blue veins. Deer resistant.

USDA Hardiness Zones 9b–10b

Bloom Period Winter–summer (February–June)

Growing Conditions Full sun (coastal), partial shade (inland); organic loamy to clayey, well-draining soils; water 1–2x/month in summer once established.

Native to open woods and sunny slopes in coastal prairies and forests, this highly variable flower often has several colors in one population. You can mass-plant a border garden with a rainbow of blues and burgundies that gets bigger and more luxuriant every year, or use it singly as a color and foliage accent. Bees follow the guide lines on the petals into the tubular flower for a reward of pollen and nectar. Inland gardens may need afternoon shade and extra summer water. To keep tidy, snip out the dead flower stalks, and trim back worn leaves to a few inches above ground. Every several years, invigorate the plants by dividing the roots after fall rains, when the rhizomes start growing little white roots. Numerous native cultivars exist, such as white-flowered 'Canyon Snow.' The commonly available Pacific Coast Hybrid (PCH) has large flowers and comes in a variety of colors.

Attracts bees and small insects; larval host for up to 2 moth species.

Farewell to Spring

Scientific Name *Clarkia amoena*

Family Evening Primrose (Onagraceae)

Plant Characteristics Annual with multibranched stems 1–3 feet tall and 1–2 feet wide; leaves linear to lance shaped, 1–2 inches long; flowers bowl shaped, 2–3 inches wide, pink to lavender, often with red spot near the middle, in tight clusters. Deer resistant.

USDA Hardiness Zones 7a–10b

Bloom Period Spring–summer (June–August)

Growing Conditions Full sun; sandy to clayey, well-draining soils; water 1–2x/month to prolong blooming.

Create your own super-bloom with mass-planted drifts of this and similar *Clarkia* species mixed with other colorful annuals; or use as a border or fill-in color accent. As the common name for the many related *Clarkia* species implies, they reach their prime in the late spring, when California Poppies and other early bloomers begin to fade. Farewell to Spring, with its showy flower clusters, as well as countless *Clarkia* cultivars and hybrids, is popular in seed mixes. In nature, petal color, spots, and size vary, so you never know exactly what will pop up from a mixed-seed pack. You can also buy seeds selected for the color and height that best fit your garden design. To create a spring–summer colorscape that gets more glamorous as the soil seed bank builds over time, mix with Globe Gilia, Baby Blue Eyes, Tidy Tips, and Tansy-Leaf Phacelia. Sow seeds directly onto coarse soils in the winter, or start in containers for patio spot color.

Attracts butterflies, bees, and other insect pollinators; larval host for 3 species of sphinx moths.

Foothill Penstemon

Scientific Name *Penstemon heterophyllus*

Family Plantain (Plantaginaceae)

Plant Characteristics Evergreen perennial with branching stems 1–3 feet tall; leaves blue-green, linear to lance shaped, 1–4 inches long; flowers tubular, 1½ inches long; petals blue, purple, magenta, in showy, spikelike clusters. Deer resistant.

USDA Hardiness Zones 7b–10b

Bloom Period Spring–summer (May–July)

Growing Conditions Full sun; coarse to clayey, well-draining soils; water 1x/month; no summer water needed once established.

Native to chaparral, foothills, and slopes of the coastal and northern mountains, this highly drought-tolerant California endemic is a star performer in habitat gardens. Each waist-high stem waves dozens of vibrant flowers and attracts mobs of butterflies, bees, and hummingbirds. Mix in some narrow-leaf milkweed for a well-rounded pollinator habitat. For a surging wave of sky-blue color, mass-plant a border or backdrop; use as a colorscape accent with Scarlet Bugler Penstemon, Western Red Columbine, Canyon (Red) Larkspur; or use as a container plant. Popular cultivars, with vibrant blue flowers and 1- to 2-foot profiles ideal for foregrounds, include 'Electric Blue,' 'Blue Springs,' and 'Margarita BOP.' Deadheading prolongs blooming.

Attracts bees, butterflies, hummingbirds, and other pollinators; larval host for Common Buckeye (Junonia coenia) *and 5 kinds of checkerspot butterflies* (Euphydryas spp.).

Globe Gilia

Scientific Name *Gilia capitata*

Family Phlox (Polemoniaceae)

Plant Characteristics Annual with slender, branching stems 6–30 inches tall and wide; leaves fernlike, with narrow lobes; flowers small, blue to pink, or white, in compact, spherical heads. Deer resistant.

USDA Hardiness Zones All zones

Bloom Period Winter–summer (February–July)

Growing Conditions Full sun and coarse, well-drained soils; water 2x/month if rains fail.

This adaptable, easy-to-grow meadow wildflower, with golf ball–size clusters of blue flowers, provides early-spring nectar for bees and butterflies. The perky flowers add a splash of color to spruce up bare spots, accent a cacti garden, or brighten a patio or walkway border. It's most dramatic when mass-planted with California Poppy, Tidy Tips, California Goldfields, and other colorful annuals, and it is a standard in pollinator seed mixes. Partner with perennials to extend seasonal color and nectar. It's a self-sowing colonizer, so once a seed bank builds in the soil, your garden will provide you with years of nectar-rich colorscaping.

Attracts bees, butterflies, and other insect pollinators; larval host for up to 4 moth species.

Hairy Gumplant

Scientific Name *Grindelia hirsutula*

Family Aster (Asteraceae)

Plant Characteristics Dense, mounding, stress-deciduous perennial with green-to-red stems, 1–2 feet tall and wide; leaves oblong to narrow, up to 4 inches long, usually serrated; daisylike flower heads 2 inches wide with 15–60 pointed, yellow rays around a yellow disk. Deer resistant.

USDA Hardiness Zones 8a–10b

Bloom Period Summer–fall (June–September)

Growing Conditions Full sun; sandy to clayey, moderate-draining soils; likes wet winters and springs but no summer water.

Native to coastal sage scrub and foothill woodlands, this hardy plant adapts well to a variety of garden conditions. Give it winter and spring moisture, along with bone-dry summers, and it will give you a mound of lemon-yellow, nectar-rich flowers from summer through fall—a perfect component of a long-season habitat landscape. Use Hairy Gumplant as a walkway border, boulder color accent, or mid-garden focal point. For habitat diversity, mix it with milkweeds, Checker Bloom, Common Woolly Sunflower, or Hummingbird Trumpet. The copious yellow flowers mature into brown seed heads, so deadheading and a seasonal trim may be needed to keep it tidy looking, but be sure to leave some seeds for birds.

Attracts bees, butterflies, and many other insects; birds eat the seeds; larval host for up to 10 moth species.

Hooker's Evening Primrose

Scientific Name *Oenothera elata*

Family Evening primrose (Onagraceae)

Plant Characteristics Herbaceous, biennial to short-lived perennial with multiple stout stems 2–6 feet tall and 3 feet wide; leaves are basal rosettes first year; stem leaves elliptical, 2–10 inches long, edges toothed or not; flowers, yellow and 2–4 inches wide, close by midday. Palatable to deer.

USDA Hardiness Zones 5a–10b

Bloom Period Summer–fall (June–September)

Growing Conditions Full sun, partial shade; well-draining, regularly moistened soils; water 1–2x/month.

With waist- to head-high leafy stems lined with bright-yellow flowers, this regal plant rules as a garden background sentinel, a border along a walkway or patio, or a color-accent patch in a habitat island. The flowers, which open at dusk and fade by the following afternoon, supply nectar for numerous pollinators, especially sphinx and other moths. In the fall, the seeds attract Lesser Goldfinches and other seed-eating birds. It favors periodically damp soils in nature but has a long taproot and is moderately drought tolerant in gardens with dappled afternoon shade. Hooker's Evening Primrose is easy to grow in garden soils, but it aggressively reseeds and may need seasonal weeding.

Attracts hummingbirds, bees, butterflies, moths; larval host for White-Lined Sphinx (Hyles lineata) and up to 14 other moth species.

Hummingbird Sage

Scientific Name *Salvia spathacea*

Family Mint (Lamiaceae)

Plant Characteristics Evergreen, mat-forming perennial 1–2 feet tall to 4 feet wide; leaves lance shaped, 3–8 inches long; magenta flowers 1 inch long on 1- to 2-foot-tall spikes. Deer resistant.

USDA Hardiness Zones 7a–10b

Bloom Period Spring (March–May)

Growing Conditions Full sun to full shade; loose, loamy, clayey, well-drained soils; water 1x/month once established.

This leafy, green mat, studded with flagpoles of red flowers, is the perfect example of a plant with specific hummingbird-syndrome adaptations (see page 15). The tubular red flowers match the length of the bird's bill, and extending stamens dust the bird's head when it plunges its bill into the flower. Often growing in shaded woodlands, this top-10 hummingbird garden selection thrives as an understory ground cover with evergreen trees and shrubs. Use it for low borders, garden foregrounds, and color fill-in accents. For color variety and a diversity of pollinators, partner it with Blue Witches, Bush Monkeyflower, and California Buckwheat, or as an understory cover with Toyon, California Buckeye, Pacific Madrone, and manzanitas. Deadhead the spent flower stems after seeds disperse, and rejuvenate old plants by cutting back to old wood in the winter. The robust 'Powerline Pink' cultivar grows 3 feet tall, with 3-foot flower stems.

Attracts hummingbirds, butterflies, and bees; larval host for up to 7 butterfly and moth species.

Indian Pink

Scientific Name *Silene laciniata* ssp. *californica*

Family Pink (Caryophyllaceae)

Plant Characteristics Straggling, taprooted perennial
with slender, leafy stems 1–3 feet tall; leaves elliptical,
1–3 inches long; flowers have 5 bright red-orange
petals with deeply cut-to-fringelike tips, in clusters
of 1–3 on branch tips. Deer resistant.

USDA Hardiness Zones 8b–10b

Bloom Period Spring–summer (April–July)

Growing Conditions Partial shade; coarse, well-draining soils;
water 2x/month in summer once established.

With brilliant red-to-orange flowers pollinated by hummingbirds
and butterflies, this native of dry, shaded oak and conifer woodlands
and chaparral adds a splash of sharp color to habitat islands, foregrounds, rock gardens, low borders, and patios. The tubular flowers
are designed for large, flying pollinators, while the sticky stems and
leaves prevent nectar thieves that are too small to pollinate (like ants
and insects) from reaching the flowers. The pollen-bearing stamens
are longer than the pistil to ensure that feeding birds and insects get
dusted with pollen. Every feature, from flower color and shape to
hairy stems and leaves, has a specific purpose: to produce and disperse
seeds. The dainty flowers provide flashy highlights when mixed with
Coyote Mint, Foothill Penstemon, Yarrow, and Blue Witches. The
similar subspecies *laciniata* is more adapted to Southern California.

*Attracts hummingbirds, butterflies, and large bees; larval host for
2 moth species.*

Leopard Lily

Scientific Name *Lilium pardalinum*

Family Lily (Liliaceae)

Plant Characteristics Winter-deciduous perennial from bulb, with stems 3–8 feet tall; leaves narrow, whorled around stem; flowers 3 inches wide, nodding; petals reflexed, orange-yellow with red spots. Deer, gophers, and chipmunks eat the bulbs.

USDA Hardiness Zones 5b–10b

Bloom Period Summer (June–July)

Growing Conditions Partial shade, tolerates soft sun; fertile, moist, well-draining soils; water 1–2x/month in summer once established.

Native to streamsides and moist meadows in the Coast Ranges, Klamath Mountains, and Sierras, this lily reaches celebrity status in your garden when up to 30 flowers dangle from the chest-high stems. Like crystal ornaments, the brilliant orange-red petals with red tips and maroon dots curve backwards to display long, spreading stamens tipped with magenta anthers. The stunning array of colors and pendant stamens serves one purpose: to attract the primary pollinators, swallowtail butterflies. In your garden, the dramatic flowers will highlight dappled backgrounds, understory groupings, and containers. After the summer spectacle of dashing color and hovering butterflies, the plant dies to the ground and goes dormant until next spring. California has 10 native lily species, many of which are propagated and available from nurseries; be sure to choose one that matches your garden habitat.

Pollinated by large butterflies, especially swallowtails and Monarchs; attracts hummingbirds.

Meadowfoam

Scientific Name *Limnanthes douglasii*

Family Meadowfoam (Limnanthaceae)

Plant Characteristics Erect annual with stems 4–12 inches tall and wide; leaves shiny green, 1–3 inches long, with finely divided leaflets; flowers 1½ inches wide; 5 yellow petals have notched, white tips. Deer resistant.

USDA Hardiness Zones 5a–10b

Bloom Period Spring–summer (March–July)

Growing Conditions Full sun to partial shade; sandy to clayey, moderate- to well-draining soils; seedlings need spring moisture.

Native to moist grasslands, meadows, open forests, and drainages from Central California to Oregon, this dainty flower creates a low-growing, two-toned carpet of color in your habitat garden. Your backyard super-bloom will attract throngs of bees, hover flies, and ladybugs, along with other pollinators and beneficial insects. Use for early companion color with deciduous shrubs such as Red Osier Dogwood, Cream Bush, or Western Mock Orange; as an understory or slope ground cover; or a mixed border with Baby Blue Eyes, California Poppies, and Farewell to Spring. Plant for spring color as a garden accent or in a patio container, alone or with taller plants. Meadowfoam readily reseeds—just rake the dried plants around to places where you want to scatter the seeds. Or sow fresh seeds in the fall or spring, and keep them moist until germination. The yellow-and-white flowers inspired its common name, Poached Egg Plant.

Attracts bees, butterflies, and many other pollinators and beneficial insects.

Narrowleaf Milkweed

Scientific Name *Asclepias fascicularis*

Family Dogbane (Apocynaceae)

Plant Characteristics Erect, herbaceous, multi-stemmed perennial 2–3 feet tall and wide; leaves linear, 2–6 inches long; small, purple-tinged-to-white flowers form dense, 5-inch-wide clusters; seed pods elongated. Deer resistant.

USDA Hardiness Zones 7a–10b

Bloom Period Spring–fall (May–October)

Growing Conditions Full sun; sandy, loamy, clayey, well-draining soils; water 2x/month once established.

Plant a milkweed in a forgotten corner or along a back wall, and you'll be a butterfly landlord all summer. With dense flower clusters and long, narrow leaves, Narrowleaf Milkweed is the most widespread milkweed in California; it's also the most important food and host species for Monarchs, and the most garden tolerant. If the leaves look ragged and chewed up, your wildscape is successful! The milky sap contains cardiac glycosides, toxins to which Monarchs are immune but which make them poisonous to predators. It spreads by rhizomes to form patches suitable for backgrounds and landscape islands. For four-season nectar plants, fill in with Hummingbird Trumpet, Coyote Mint, Foothill Penstemon, Bush Monkeyflower, Canyon (Red) Larkspur, and buckwheats. A deep taproot allows it to survive droughts, but extra summer water prolongs blooming. The other California milkweeds have the same garden uses and habitat value.

Attracts butterflies, bees, and other pollinators; larval host for Monarch and Queen Butterflies and up to 4 moth species.

Redwood Sorrel

Scientific Name *Oxalis oregana*

Family Oxalis (Oxalidaceae)

Plant Characteristics Perennial ground cover, with spreading stems, up to 6–12 inches tall and 6 feet wide; dark-green leaves have 3 heart-shaped leaflets; flowers 1 inch wide with 5 pink-to-white petals, often with red lines. Deer resistant.

USDA Hardiness Zones 7b–9b

Bloom Period Winter–fall (February–September)

Growing Conditions Full or bright shade; rich, humous, well-draining soils; requires summer water.

This dense ground cover with shamrock-like leaves and petite flowers thrives in moist conifer forests along the coast—and in those hard-to-fill-shady spots in your habitat garden. As an understory foliage fill-in, it competes well with tree roots. Use it as a walkway border, boulder accent, or foliage cover with Western Red Columbine or Leopard Lilies. To inhibit self-pollination, oxalis flowers have styles either longer or shorter than their pollen-bearing anthers; this way, insects always transfer pollen to a different flower. The plant spreads by rhizomes to create a dense blanket of foliage and flower color that extends for four seasons in frost-free regions. It performs best in rich, moist soils, and though drought tolerant, it appreciates extra summer water in exposed locations if it begins look ragged. It can be aggressive in garden soils, but the shallow rhizomes are easy to control.

Pollinated by bees and flies; attracts butterflies and other insects; larval host for up to 4 moth species.

Sacred Datura

Scientific Name *Datura wrightii*

Family Nightshade (Solanaceae)

Plant Characteristics Robust, mounding, spreading, herbaceous perennial 2–4 feet tall and 6–8 feet wide; gray-green, hairy, triangular leaves up to 6 inches long; flowers white, trumpet shaped, 6–8 inches wide; fruit spiny, egg shaped. All parts are poisonous to ingest or handle. Deer resistant.

USDA Hardiness Zones 6a–11a

Bloom Period Spring–fall (April–November)

Growing Conditions Full sun, partial shade; dry, coarse, well-draining soils; water 1x/month.

A dozen eye-popping, fragrant, white flowers, nestled in gray-green foliage, may cover this sprawling plant every morning; then they fade by noon. Like most plants with fragrant, white flowers, Sacred Datura opens at night for moth pollination, so it's ideal for a nocturnal (or moon) garden. Sphinx moths pollinate them; come morning, bees dive in for the addictive, hallucinogenic nectar. Give daturas lots of room to spread against a wall, in a neglected corner, or as a back-ground border. Deadhead unless you want seedlings. Plant away from human contact, and wear protective clothing when pruning, or you may have wild dreams—or much worse. Also called Jimsonweed (or, less commonly, Jamestown Weed) because it caused hallucinations and mass confusion in the colonial settlement of Jamestown, Virginia.

Attracts sphinx moths, bees, and other pollinators; larval host for up to 7 moth species.

213

Scarlet Bugler Penstemon

Scientific Name *Penstemon centranthifolius*

Family Plantain (Plantaginaceae)

Plant Characteristics Perennial evergreen with 1 to 2-foot-tall/wide clumps and many 2- to 4-foot-tall flower stems; lance-shaped leaves in dense basal clump, opposite on stems; flowers brilliant red, tubular, in dense spikes. Emerging flower stems palatable to deer.

USDA Hardiness Zones 8b–10b

Bloom Period Spring–summer (March–July)

Growing Conditions Full sun; coarse, well-draining soils; summer water 1x/month in summer once established.

Its lush, green, leafy mounds punctuated with dozens of tall stems waving hundreds of scarlet flowers, this flamboyant penstemon will be the floral highlight of your garden all spring, especially for the hummingbirds. Native to coastal chaparral and oak woodlands from the North Coastal Ranges southward, Scarlet Bugler Penstemon is drought tolerant, but a little extra summer water helps keep it vibrant. Hummingbirds mob the nectar-rich flowers, and butterflies and large bees aren't bashful about joining the buffet. Use it as a midgarden focal point, cactus or rock-garden accent, border planting, or container plant. For extended seasonal color and pollinator diversity, pair it with Foothill Penstemon, California Buckwheat, Golden Yarrow, and milkweeds. Deadhead after the seeds disperse.

Attracts hummingbirds, bumblebees, and butterflies; larval host for Common Buckeye (Junonia coenia) *and checkerspot* (Euphydryas spp.) *butterflies, plus 3 moth species.*

Seaside Daisy

Scientific Name *Erigeron glaucus*

Family Aster (Asteraceae)

Plant Characteristics Herbaceous perennial with spreading, rhizomatous stems 1 foot tall and 2 feet wide; leaves dark green, spoon shaped, 1–5 inches long; flower head 1–2 inches wide, rays lavender to magenta and white, disk yellow. Deer resistant.

USDA Hardiness Zones 8b–10b

Bloom Period Spring–fall (April–September)

Growing Conditions Full sun (coastal), partial shade (inland); sandy, clayey, well-draining soils; water 2x/month in summer once established.

With up to 300 narrow lavender rays surrounding a large yellow disk, this nectar-rich flower keeps the pollinators busy spring through summer. The roots spread to form dense colonies that are ideal for garden accents, foregrounds, and containers. To increase pollinator diversity, plant a border with a mix of Hummingbird Trumpet, Yarrow, Coast Buckwheat, or Spreading Coastal Gumplant. Native to the coast, where cool breezes bring relief on hot, sunny days, this perky plant needs heat and sun protection, along with extra summer water, to perform well in inland gardens. Nurseries carry a number of cultivars in various colors and sizes. 'Bountiful,' 'Cape Sebastian,' 'Sea Breeze,' 'Arthur Menzies,' and 'Wayne Roderick' (a heat-tolerant, long-blooming hybrid) are among the popular selections. Deadhead for prolonged blooming and a tidy look.

Attracts butterflies, bees, and other pollinators; larval host for up 11 butterfly and moth species.

Self-Heal

Scientific Name *Prunella vulgaris*

Family Mint (Laminaceae)

Plant Characteristics Herbaceous, perennial ground
cover with spreading, rooting stems 3–16 inches high;
leaves lance shaped, 1–3 inches long; tubular flowers
pink, purple, ¾ inch long, upper lip hooded, lower lip
has 3 lobes in stout terminal spikes. Deer resistant.

USDA Hardiness Zones 5a–9a

Bloom Period Summer (June–August)

Growing Conditions Full sun, partial shade; damp, sandy, loamy,
well-draining soils; likes summer moisture.

With a worldwide distribution, this little mint has been a popular
edible and medicinal herb in many cultures for centuries. In your
pollinator garden, it thrives in periodically moist soils, sun, or partial
shade. The Xerces Society lists 10 butterfly, moth, and bee genera
that forage on the plant. It spreads by rooting stems, so it's well suited
as a ground cover, border or edge plant, garden accent, or addition
to a mowed eco-lawn or living-roof garden. Its summer-long blooms
keep the pollinators coming back and add ground-level floral interest
to trimmed-up shrubs and small trees, walkways, and containers. If
you can't find starter plants, sow seeds in the spring, gently pressing
them into the soil. Self-Heal spreads aggressively and can be divided.
Replant plugs 6–12 inches apart.

Attracts bees, butterflies, and many other pollinators; birds eat seeds.

Showy Milkweed

Scientific Name *Asclepias speciosa*

Family Dogbane (Apocynaceae)

Plant Characteristics Upright, herbaceous perennial 2–4 feet tall; large, oval blue-green leaves have hairy undersides; star-shaped, pinkish-white flowers grow in dense spherical clusters 4–5 inches wide; fruit a 4-inch, pointed pod. Deer and rabbit resistant.

USDA Hardiness Zones 3a–9b

Bloom Period Summer (June–July)

Growing Conditions Full sun; sandy, clayey, loamy, well-draining soils; water 2x/month in summer once established.

Want Monarch Butterflies? Plant milkweeds. Native to meadows, valleys, and roadsides in the Coast Ranges and Sierras, Showy Milkweed earns its common name. Tall stems covered with large, broad leaves and showy clusters of pinkish flowers are followed by hornlike pods that split open and release seeds with feathery tails. With a long taproot, this milkweed is moderately drought tolerant. It grows in a variety of soil types, but it needs full sun. For habitat diversity, plant it with Oregon Grape, buckwheats, sunflowers, and Hummingbird Trumpet, and you'll attract butterflies, hummingbirds, and large and small bees. This and other milkweed species are the most important nectar and host plants for Monarch Butterflies, and are critical for their survival. The milky sap contains cardiac glycosides, toxins to which Monarchs are immune but which make them poisonous to predators.

Attracts butterflies, bees, and many other insect pollinators; larval host for Monarch (Danaus plexippus) and Queen (Danaus gilippus) Butterflies and 2 tiger moth species.

Spreading Coastal Gumplant

Scientific Name *Grindelia stricta* var. *platyphylla*

Family Aster (Asteraceae)

Plant Characteristics Evergreen perennial with spreading, rooting stems 1 foot tall and 3 feet wide; leaves oblong, fleshy; flower head yellow, 2 inches wide; bud has white, gummy resin. Deer resistant.

USDA Hardiness Zones 9a–10b

Bloom Period Spring–fall (May–October)

Growing Conditions Full sun (coastal), partial shade (inland); sandy, coarse, well-draining soils; water 2–3x/month in summer.

Golden-yellow flowers cover this spreading ground cover much of the year, making it a valuable addition to a pollinator garden. Native to coastal areas, it adapts well to inland gardens with partial shade and extra summer water. The rooting stems will continue to spread and form a solid mat of green and gold. Use it as a foreground, border, or fill-in plant together with Seaside Daisy, Hummingbird Sage, or midsize perennials. With its long blooming season, it will have many spent brown heads mixed with the vibrant flowers, so deadhead to keep it tidy. But the seed-eating birds will thank you for leaving a few seed heads.

Attracts bees, butterflies, and other insects; birds eat the seeds; larval host for up to 10 moth species.

Sulphur Buckwheat

Scientific Name *Eriogonum umbellatum*

Family Buckwheat (Polygonaceae)

Plant Characteristics Evergreen perennial forming dense mats to 3 feet wide; leaves gray-green, oval, 1 inch long; flowers small, yellow to cream or reddish, in dense clusters on 6- to 9-inch-tall stalks. Deer resistant.

USDA Hardiness Zones 5a–10a

Bloom Period Winter–summer (February–June)

Growing Conditions Full sun, partial shade; coarse, well-draining soils; summer water 1–3x/month once established.

With 3-inch-wide clusters of lemon-yellow (or sometimes creamy white) flowers hovering over a green mat of leafy stems, this wide-ranging buckwheat dazzles any garden. Insect pollinators find the long-blooming flowers an irresistible source of nectar and pollen. And the plants keep giving, providing both pollinator food, and garden color when the flowers fade to russet heads. Seed-eating birds flock to the garden for winter treats. Use as a ground cover, foreground, or mixed border, or as a boulder, walkway, or patio accent. For pollinator and color diversity, mix with Yarrow, Hummingbird Trumpet, Blue-Eyed Grass, and Coyote Mint. Growers have selected numerous cultivars from the 25 varieties that naturally occur in California, mostly in mountain habitats. The versatile 'Shasta Sulphur' is one of the top garden performers throughout the state.

Attracts butterflies, bees, and other pollinators; birds eat the seeds; larval host for up to 47 butterflies and moths.

Tansy-Leaf Phacelia

Scientific Name *Phacelia tanacetifolia*

Family Waterleaf (Hydrophyllaceae)

Plant Characteristics Annual with stout, densely leafy, hairy stems 3–4 feet tall; leaves oval, 1–8 inches long, fernlike, with lacy, deeply cut leaflets; flowers blue, small, tubular, in densely coiled clusters on branching stem ends. Deer resistant.

USDA Hardiness Zones 5a–10b

Bloom Period Spring (March–May)

Growing Conditions Full sun, partial shade; coarse, well-draining soils; water if winter moisture fails.

This drought-tolerant annual—native to chaparral, valley grasslands, and foothills—earns a spot on the top-20 list of plants for honeybees. Famous for its copious early-spring nectar and pollen production, it is planted in the Midwest, as well as in Europe, as an agriculture cover crop, or "bee pasture." In home gardens, it's a superstore for bees, bumblebees, and other beneficial native pollinators. Waist high, with dense, lacy foliage and topped with coiling clusters of small, blue flowers, it will dominate a walkway border, background planting, or mass-planted garden island. It fades in early summer, so remove spent plants to make way for the succession of summer perennial flowers. Often included in seed mixes; sow in the fall for spring germination, and water if winter rains fail.

Highly attractive to bees, butterflies, and other insect pollinators; larval host for up to 9 moth species.

Tidy Tips

Scientific Name *Layia platyglossa*

Family Aster (Asteraceae)

Plant Characteristics Annual with slender stems ½ foot–2 feet tall; lance-shaped leaves up to 4 inches long; daisylike flower head 2 inches wide, rays yellow with scalloped white margins, yellow-orange disk. Palatable to deer.

USDA Hardiness Zones All zones

Bloom Period Winter–spring (February–March)

Growing Conditions Full sun; well-draining soils; no extra water.

Early and long blooming, this multicolored meadow flower creates an ethereal dance between butterflies and flowers waving in the breeze. For visual appeal, both in terms of color and pollinators, plant along walkway and patio borders, as boulder accents, and for early-season fill-in color with summer perennials. A patch, slope, or mass planting of annuals is most spectacular when naturalized with friends such as California Poppy, Baby Blue Eyes, California Goldfields, and Globe Gilia, all species commonly included in wildflower seed mixes. Tidy Tips readily reseeds; you can also sow in the fall by gently pressing the seeds directly into the soil. After it's germinated by winter rains, thin or transplant it as needed. Extra water in dry years increases both germination and blooming.

Attracts butterflies, bees, and other insect pollinators.

Western Pearly Everlasting

Scientific Name *Anaphalis margaritacea*

Family Aster (Asteraceae)

Plant Characteristics Upright, clump-forming, herbaceous perennial 1–2 feet tall; slender leaves are covered with white, woolly hairs on undersides; male and female flowers occupy separate plants; flower heads form tight clusters of papery, pearly-white bracts surrounding tiny, yellow disk flowers. Deer resistant.

USDA Hardiness Zones 3a–10a

Bloom Period Summer–fall (June–September)

Growing Conditions Full sun, partial shade; needs coarse, well-draining soils; water max 2x/month in summer once established.

Widespread from chaparral, grasslands, and foothill woodlands to the northern and Sierra conifer forests, this easy-to-grow plant stakes its claim as a long-lasting flowering accent. With mounds of silvery, gray-green leaves and dense clusters of striking white and yellow flowers, it's well suited as part of a garden foreground, border garden, or mixed-understory planting. For a dramatic colorscape, pair with bright, similarly sized flowers such as Coyote Mint, Hairy Gumplant, Blue-Eyed Grass, and Seaside Daisy. It spreads by stolons and, under optimum conditions, can form colonies. Propagate by division, or sow seeds on bare ground after the last frost. The plant yields attractive cut flowers, but leave some to provide late-season nectar and pollen for bees, butterflies, moths, and other insects.

Attracts butterflies, moths, bees, and other insect pollinators; larval host plant for American Lady (Vanessa virginiensis) and Painted Lady (Vanessa cardui) Butterflies and up to 10 moth species.

Western Red Columbine

Scientific Name *Aquilegia formosa*

Family Buttercup (Ranunculaceae)

Plant Characteristics Erect, herbaceous perennial with multiple stems 2-3 feet tall; 2-3 feet wide; compound leaves have 3 fan-shaped leaflets; flowers dangle, with showy yellow stamens and red petals forming long spurs. Deer resistant.

USDA Hardiness Zones 7a–10a

Bloom Period Spring–fall (April–October)

Growing Conditions Full sun (coastal), partial shade (inland); moist, medium-draining soils; water 1x/month (summer) once established.

Protect this delicate plant from sunbaked, arid locations; give it regularly moistened (but not waterlogged) soil and dappled afternoon light; and marvel at its abundant crimson flowers and fine-textured foliage. Like fairy lanterns, the dangling flowers seem to float on a cloud of light-green leaves. Hummingbirds, the designated pollinators, feast on the nectar hidden in the flowers' long spurs, along with butterflies and bumblebees. The mounding plants make a colorful background, patio or poolside container planting, color accent for a dappled corner, or mixed planting with other partial-shade plants like Blue-eyed Grass, Leopard Lily, Indian Pink, or Checker Bloom. To prolong blooming, deadhead spent flowers, or leave them to self-sow in your garden.

Attracts hummingbirds, butterflies, bees, and other pollinators; larval host for up to 5 moth species.

Yarrow

Scientific Name *Achillea millefolium*

Family Aster (Asteraceae)

Plant Characteristics Herbaceous, rhizomatous perennial with a dense basal rosette and multiple leafy flower stems; leaves compound, fernlike; small, white-to-pink flowers form dense, flat-topped clusters on 1- to 3-foot-tall stalks. Deer and rabbit resistant.

USDA Hardiness Zones 5b–10b

Bloom Period Spring–summer (April–August)

Growing Conditions Full sun (coastal), partial shade (inland); sandy, loamy, clayey, well-draining soils; water 1x/week once established.

Tough and adaptable, Yarrow grows from alpine slopes to deserts in California, and worldwide. The 3- to 5-inch-wide flower clusters are a nectar bonanza for butterflies, bees, and all manner of insects. Native flies—nature's second-most important pollinators after bees—are major visitors. With dense rosettes of aromatic, fernlike leaves, Yarrow spreads by rhizomes, and in loose soil it can form an attractive ground cover or border accent with dozens of flower stalks. For pollinator diversity, mix with other foliage-textured wildflowers, such as Seaside Daisy, Coyote Mint, Blue-Eyed Grass, or Foothill Penstemon, depending on your garden habitat. Cultivars include yellow and pink, though some, especially red, have diminished pollinator appeal, so try to stick with the true species. Deadhead to prolong blooming. Hot, sunny sites may need extra water.

Attracts butterflies, bees, native flies, and other insect pollinators; larval host for up to 15 moth species.

Yellow Sand-Verbena

Scientific Name *Abronia latifolia*

Family Four O'Clock (Nyctaginaceae)

Plant Characteristics Beach perennial with prostrate, branching, mat-forming stems 2–6 feet long; leaves oval to rounded, fleshy, 1–2 inches long; small, yellow flowers form spherical clusters on 5-inch-long stems. Deer resistant.

USDA Hardiness Zones 9b–10b

Bloom Period Spring–fall (March–October)

Growing Conditions Full sun; well-draining, pure-sand soils; only occasional summer water once established.

Occurring on sandy beaches and scrublands within 50 yards of the surf, this tough coastal native thrives from Santa Barbara to Canada, but it will thrive in your habitat garden only if you can replicate its natural habitat of pure sand with no organic material. The balls of lemon-yellow flowers will transform a coastal garden or sandy bluff into a butterfly theme park with a ground cover of deep-rooted, leafy mats. For color and habitat diversity, mix Yellow Sand-Verbena with similar low-growing, sand-tolerant plants such as Seaside Daisy, Spreading Coastal Gumplant, Coast Buckwheat, Seaside Woolly Sunflower, and Coyote Brush. It's an excellent way to stabilize a sandy lot or slope. Don't overwater with fresh water—this plant is adapted to survive on salt spray. Propagate by seeds sown in fall.

Attracts butterflies, bees, and other insect pollinators; larval host for White-Lined Sphinx Moth (Hyles lineata) and up to 3 other moth species.

California Fescue

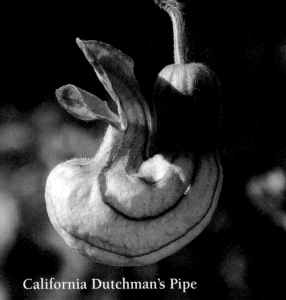

California Dutchman's Pipe

Vines & Grasses

Virgin's Bower Clematis

Deer Grass

Anacapa Pink Island Morning Glory

California Wild Grape

Combine a vine and a trellis, and what do you get? A hanging garden that will decorate a barren wall or add leafy texture to a fence. Robust climbing vines can create a shady patio shelter and provide shelter and nesting for birds. Delicate vines accent smaller oval or rock gardens.

With showy, feathery seed heads and a vaselike spray of leaf blades, many bunchgrasses have highly ornamental qualities. As keystone plants in the food chain, they provide food, shelter, and nesting sites; build soil; and prevent erosion. Caterpillars eat the blades, birds eat the seeds, and some bees overwinter in the clump stubble.

Pink Honeysuckle

Canyon Prince Wild Rye

239

Anacapa Pink Island Morning Glory

Scientific Name *Calystegia macrostegia* 'Anacapa Pink'

Family Morning glory (Convolvulaceae)

Plant Characteristics Climbing, twining, semievergreen vine up to 25 feet long and 6 feet wide; leaves triangular, 4 inches wide; white, trumpet-shaped flowers 3 inches wide with pale-pink streaks. Deer resistant.

USDA Hardiness Zones 7b–10b

Bloom Period Winter–summer (February–August)

Growing Conditions Full sun (coastal), partial shade (inland); coarse, well-draining soils; summer water 1x/week once established.

Though six varieties of Island Morning Glories are common along the southern coast, this popular horticultural selection from Anacapa Island grows like gangbusters in coastal settings. Inland, it performs best with afternoon shade and extra water. Its pizzazz comes from the abundance of showy, extra-large, white- and pink-lined flowers and dense foliage that cover the aggressive, twining stems. The flowers particularly attract moths and bees, nature's most prolific pollinators. Use it to cover walls, fences, and arbors, or as a slope ground cover. Known for their vigorous growth, Island Morning Glories tend to get out of hand and pop up uninvited, especially in garden soil, so prune to size in winter and weed out unwanted seedlings.

Attracts butterflies, bees, and other insect pollinators; larval host for up to 3 moth species.

California Dutchman's Pipe

Scientific Name *Aristolochia californica*

Family Pipevine (Aristolochiaceae)

Plant Characteristics Twining vine from rhizome with woody stem up to 20 feet long; leaves deciduous, heart shaped; flowers greenish brown, purple striped, J shaped, 1 inch long. Deer resistant.

USDA Hardiness Zones 8a–10b

Bloom Period Winter–spring (January–April)

Growing Conditions Partial shade; moderate- to well-draining soils; moderate water 1x/week in summer once established.

Native to streambanks in chaparral, foothill woodlands, and mixed forests, this pipevine has bizarre flowers—which by themselves are enough to justify a place in your pollinator garden. But they're more than a conversation starter: though California Dutchman's Pipe is pollinated by fungus gnats attracted to its musty odor, the leaves attract the gorgeous Pipevine Swallowtail Butterfly. Look for the black caterpillars with red spikes munching away at the leaves—they ingest a poison that protects them and the adults from hungry birds. In early spring, the purple-lined flowers cover the vine profusely, and by summer the dangling seed capsules look like miniature lanterns. Once established, this fast grower will spread as a scrambling ground cover with rooting stems and climb into shrubs, trees, fences, and arbors. Better yet, use it as a seasonal accent on a trellis placed close enough to observe the intriguing flowers and butterfly life cycle, from eggs to adults.

Larval host for Pipevine Swallowtail Butterfly (Battus philenor).

California Fescue

Scientific Name *Festuca californica*

Family Grass (Poaceae)

Plant Characteristics Cool-season perennial bunch-grass, evergreen on coast; dense clumps of arching, blue-gray leaves 2–3 feet tall, 1–2 feet wide; flower spikes and seed heads top stems 2–3 feet above foliage. Deer resistant.

USDA Hardiness Zones 7a–11a

Bloom Period Spring–summer (May–June)

Growing Conditions Full sun (coastal), partial shade (interior); clayey to loamy, well-draining soils; summer water 1–3x/month once established.

Designated by the UC Davis Arboretum as a Landscape All Star, this native to open woodlands fills many roles in a habitat garden. Use it as a border, a shade-tolerant understory highlight, or a specimen or container plant; you can also mass-plant it in drifts with annuals for colorscaping. The arching fountain of blue-gray blades and airy spikes of reddish flowers (or brown seeds) provides a dramatic garden accent. California Fescue is evergreen in frost-free coastal gardens and herbaceous inland, but it's root hardy to 0°F. Extra summer water keeps it lush. Grasses in habitat gardens are an important source of larval food and overwintering habitat for caterpillars and bees, so delay shearing the clump until spring growth begins. With many cultivars available, choose one that's well suited to your area.

Provides overwintering habitat for bees; birds eat the seeds; larval host for up to 8 butterfly and moth species.

California Wild Grape

Scientific Name *Vitis californica*

Family Grape (Vitaceae)

Plant Characteristics Deciduous, multibranched, high-climbing vine with tendrils; robust stems reach 30–50 feet long and wide; leaves silvery, broad, lobed, red in fall; flowers not showy; fruit is clusters of juicy black grapes. Palatable to deer.

USDA Hardiness Zones 8b–10b

Bloom Period Spring–summer (May–June); fruit: July–September

Growing Conditions Full sun, partial shade; well-draining soils; water 1x/month once established.

This robust, fast-growing grape brings three-season interest to your wildlife-friendly landscape. Bees, butterflies, and other pollinators feed on the tiny spring flowers; dense foliage provides cover for nesting birds; the sweet fruit feeds birds, butterflies, and other pollinators through the summer; and the dark-red leaves lend autumn color. You can train it to trail over a wall or cover fence, use it as a ground cover or espalier, or place it on a wire grid as a garden background, facade, or screen. But grapes come with caveats. The aggressive branches need regular winter pruning to keep within design boundaries; the plants will overtake shrubs, trees, or a small trellis; and fallen fruit can make a mess on walkways and patios. The 'Roger's Red' hybrid and several cultivars produce brilliant fall colors.

Attracts bees and other pollinators; provides cover and food for birds; larval host for up to 32 species of moths.

Canyon Prince Wild Rye

Scientific Name *Leymus condensatus* 'Canyon Prince'

Family Grass (Poaceae)

Plant Characteristics Clumping, cool-season, perennial, evergreen grass 2–5 feet tall, spreads 3–4 feet wide by rhizomes; leaf blades blue-gray, arching; tan flowers top spikes 1–2 feet above foliage. Deer resistant.

USDA Hardiness Zones 7b–10b

Bloom Period Summer (June–August)

Growing Conditions Performs best in full sun, tolerates partial shade; sandy, clayey, well-draining soils; water 1x/month in summer once established.

This cultivar from the larger, green-leaved parent species in the Channel Islands was selected for its silvery, blue-gray leaves and compact form. The tall, arching leaf blades and summer seed plumes add vertical garden interest as well as a color contrast to green foliated plants. Use as a slope, meadow, or wall accent; a walkway border; a background planting; or a patio container planting. To tidy up and rejuvenate, cut back in summer before new growth emerges. Cool-season grasses grow in the spring and fall (65°–80°F), with a period of summer dormancy. Extra spring water in dry regions promotes lush growth, but overwatering makes it lank. Grasses are an important element in a pollinator garden, providing larval food and overwintering habitat for caterpillars and bees. The Xerces Society advises planting at least two bunchgrasses in a habitat garden.

Provides overwintering habitat for bees; birds eat the seeds; larval host for up to 12 moth species.

Deer Grass

Scientific Name *Muhlenbergia rigens*

Family Grass (Poaceae)

Plant Characteristics Mounding, perennial, warm-season, semievergreen bunchgrass 2–5 feet tall and wide; blades long, narrow, and arching, gray green in summer, brown during winter dormancy; straw-colored flowers rest on 3- to 4-foot-tall spikes. Deer resistant, but rabbits may eat young plants.

USDA Hardiness Zones 6a–10b

Bloom Period Summer–fall (June–September)

Growing Conditions Full sun, tolerates partial shade with slower growth; coarse, well-draining soils; water 1x/week in summer until established to speed growth.

With varying summer and winter foliage colors and fall plumes of straw-colored flowers, deer grass provides garden texture and color for most of the year. It reaches full size in two growing seasons and is noninvasive and long-lived. Its large size suits it to backgrounds, mass plantings, or walkway borders, or to draping its arching leaves over a retaining wall. Though the flowers are wind pollinated, bunch-grasses are important components of a pollinator garden. Caterpillars feed on the leaves, and the dense basal tuft provides nesting and overwinter shelter for bumblebees and moth larvae, so resist pruning the dormant winter clumps until spring. Regenerate every 2–3 years by trimming to 3 inches; this way, the new growth won't have to fight through the dead stubble. Deer grass needs little supplemental water after the first year, but extra summer water helps keep it lush.

Provides nesting and overwintering habitat for bees, moth larvae, and other insect pollinators; larval host for California Ringlet (Coenonympha tullia californica), Umber Skipper (Poanes melane), and satyrid butterflies (subfamily Satyrinae).

Mendocino Leafy Reed Grass

Scientific Name *Calamagrostis foliosa*

Family Grass (Poaceae)

Plant Characteristics Dense-mounding, cool season, evergreen bunchgrass 1–2 feet tall and wide; arching, blue-green leaf blades; flower spikelets and seeds sit atop tall, nodding stems. Deer resistant.

USDA Hardiness Zones 8a–10b

Bloom Period Spring–winter (May–November)

Growing Conditions Full sun (coastal), partial shade (inland); well-draining soils; water 1x/week in summer once established.

Rare in nature on the northern coast but common in nurseries, this handsome bunchgrass has arching, leafy mounds with nodding spikes of purplish flowers in the spring and golden seed plumes through the fall. The fountain of glowing, backlighted seeds makes an eye-catching specimen, rock accent, garden or walkway border, under-story ground cover, or pattern planting. The foliage contrasts well with evergreens like Toyon and manzanita and ceanothus selections. For colorscaping, partner with Hummingbird Trumpet, Yarrow, and Blue-Eyed Grass. Though wind pollinated, grasses provide larval food and overwintering habitat for caterpillars and bees. Extra water improves appearance. Unlike many bunchgrasses, Mendocino Leafy Reed Grass responds poorly to shearing; instead, remove thatch with hard raking, and rejuvenate every 3–5 years via clump division.

Provides overwintering habitat for bees and caterpillars; larval host for Arctic Skipper Butterfly (Carterocephalus palaemon).

Pink Honeysuckle

Scientific Name *Lonicera hispidula*

Family Honeysuckle (Caprifoliaceae)

Plant Characteristics Sprawling, shrubby, deciduous vine with slender stems 6–20 feet long; leaves oblong, opposite along stem; flowers hairy, pink, tubular, with 2 lips curled backwards; fruit is clusters of red berries. Deer resistant.

USDA Hardiness Zones 8a–11a

Bloom Period Spring–summer (April–July); fruit: September

Growing Conditions Full sun, partial shade; coarse, clayey, well-draining soils; water 1x/month once established.

Native to foothills understory, thickets, and open areas, this mild-mannered honeysuckle never trespasses in garden settings. The small clusters of pink flowers are hummingbird favorites, and birds relish the red berries. Let this informal wildscape vine twine through shrubs for a seasonal floral and fruit color accent, or train it against a trellis, fence, or wall. It will sprawl as an understory ground cover or mound up for a multibranched, shrubby fill-in. Like many vines that climb for the sun, it likes shady roots, so mulch if needed. In hot locations, it appreciates afternoon shade and extra summer water. Also called Hairy Honeysuckle.

Attracts hummingbirds, bees, and butterflies; provides cover and food for birds; larval host for Chalcedon Checkerspot Butterfly (Euphydryas chalcedona) *and up to 23 moths.*

Virgin's Bower Clematis

Scientific Name *Clematis ligusticifolia*

Family Buttercup (Ranunculaceae)

Plant Characteristics Deciduous, perennial vine with twining stems 8–20 feet long; compound leaves have 5–7 leaflets; flowers 1 inch wide, creamy white with showy stamens, in dense clusters; fruit has feathery tails; male and female plants separate. Deer resistant.

USDA Hardiness Zones 5a–10b

Bloom Period Summer–fall (June–September)

Growing Conditions Full sun, partial shade; coarse, loamy, medium- to well-draining soils; water 1–2x/month in summer once established.

Native to streamsides and moist hills in grasslands and forests from the Coast Ranges to the Sierra foothills, this vine naturally twines through shrubs and trees to reach the sun, leaving its roots shaded. Mulch the roots in your garden, and clusters of starburst flowers will bloom profusely all summer, followed by a mass of ornamental, feathery seed plumes. Train over a trellis, pergola, or fence, or let it naturally climb through early-blooming shrubs and trees for a summer color accent. The dense foliage provides cover for nesting birds, and the flowers attract moths and other pollinators. Prune during winter dormancy; rejuvenate with severe pruning every 3–5 years. The more drought-tolerant Chaparral Clematis (*C. lasiantha*) has slightly larger flowers, as well as similar landscape uses, and it blooms from winter to spring.

Attracts butterflies, moths, bees; provides cover for birds; larval host for Fatal Metalmark Butterfly (Calephelis nemesis) and up to 8 moth species.

Garden Plants for Butterflies

259

Garden Plants for Bees

TREES & SHRUBS

WILDFLOWERS

Container Gardening for Pollinators

SHRUBS

WILDFLOWERS

263

Bird Food & Nesting Plants

TREES

COMMON NAME	SCIENTIFIC NAME
Blue Elderberry pg. 39	*Sambucus nigra* ssp. *cerulea*
California Bay pg. 41	*Umbellularia californica*
Hollyleaf Cherry pg. 45	*Prunus ilicifolia* ssp. *ilicifolia*
Pacific Wax Myrtle pg. 49	*Morella californica*

SHRUBS

COMMON NAME	SCIENTIFIC NAME
California Coffeeberry pg. 65	*Frangula californica*
Chokecherry pg. 81	*Prunus virginiana*
Common Snowberry pg. 85	*Symphoricarpos albus* var. *laevigatus*
Currants & Gooseberries pgs. 77, 95, 99, 125	*Ribes* spp.
Manzanitas pgs. 91, 105	*Arctostaphylos* spp.
Oregon Grape pg. 119	*Berberis aquifolium*
Red Osier Dogwood pg. 127	*Cornus sericea*
Toyon pg. 137	*Heteromeles arbutifolia*
Twinberry Honeysuckle pg. 139	*Lonicera involucrata* var. *ledebourii*

WILDFLOWERS & VINES

COMMON NAME	SCIENTIFIC NAME
Buckwheats pgs. 63, 117, 131, 179, 225	*Eriogonum* spp.
Common Sunflower pg. 183	*Helianthus annuus*
California Wild Grape pg. 247	*Vitis californica*

Hummingbird Plants

SHRUBS

COMMON NAME	SCIENTIFIC NAME
Chapparal Currant pg. 77	*Ribes malvaceum*
Fuchsia-Flowered Gooseberry pg. 95	*Ribes speciosum*
Heartleaf Keckiella pg. 103	*Keckiella cordifolia*
Hummingbird Trumpet pg. 107	*Epilobium canum*
Island Snapdragon pg. 111	*Gambelia speciosa*
Manzanitas pgs. 91, 105	*Arctostaphylos* spp.
Pink-Flowering Currant pg. 125	*Ribes sanguineum*
Western Spirea pg. 147	*Spiraea douglasii var. glutinosum*

WILDFLOWERS & VINES

COMMON NAME	SCIENTIFIC NAME
Canyon (Red) Larkspur pg. 171	*Delphinium nudicaule*
Coyote Mint pg. 187	*Monardella villosa*
Hummingbird Sage pg. 201	*Salvia spathacea*
Pink Honeysuckle pg. 255	*Lonicera hispidula*
Scarlet Bugler Penstemon pg. 215	*Penstemon centranthifolius*
Western Red Columbine pg. 233	*Aquilegia formosa*

Plant Landscape Applications

GROUND COVERS

Plants suitable for ground covers typically are low growing, with sprawling or rooting stems, or spread by rhizomes. Some erect species have low-growing cultivars. Pattern planting over open ground is also effective, especially with grasses.

SHRUBS

COMMON NAME	SCIENTIFIC NAME
California Buckwheat pg. 63	Eriogonum fasciculatum cultivars
California Coffeeberry pg. 65	Frangula californica cultivars
Chamise pg. 75	Adenostoma fasciculatum cultivars
Coyote Brush pg. 87	Baccharis pilularis ssp. pilularis 'Pigeon Point'
Fragrant Sumac pg. 93	Rhus aromatica
Golden Yarrow pg. 101	Eriophyllum confertiflorum
Heartleaf Keckiella pg. 103	Keckiella cordifolia
Hummingbird Trumpet pg. 107	Epilobium canum
Oregon Grape pg. 119	Berberis aquifolium 'Compacta'
Our Lord's Candle pg. 121	Hesperoyucca whipplei
Salal pg. 129	Gaultheria shallon
Silver Bush Lupine pg. 133	Lupinus albifrons
Yankee Point Ceanothus pg. 151	Ceanothus griseus 'Yankee Point'

WILDFLOWERS

COMMON NAME	SCIENTIFIC NAME
California Golden Violet pg. 165	Viola pedunculata
Coast Aster pg. 177	Symphyotrichum chilense cultivars
Coast Buckwheat pg. 179	Eriogonum latifolium
Coyote Mint pg. 187	Monardella villosa
Hummingbird Sage pg. 201	Salvia spathacea
Redwood Sorrel pg. 211	Oxalis oregana
Self-Heal pg. 219	Prunella vulgaris
Spreading Coastal Gumplant pg. 223	Grindelia stricta var. platyphylla
Sulphur Buckwheat pg. 225	Eriogonum umbellatum
Yarrow pg. 235	Achillea millefolium
Yellow Sand-Verbena pg. 237	Abronia latifolia

VINES & GRASSES

COMMON NAME	SCIENTIFIC NAME
Anacapa Pink Island Morning Glory pg. 241	*Calystegia macrostegia* 'Anacapa Pink'
California Dutchman's Pipe pg. 243	*Aristolochia californica*
Canyon Prince Wild Rye pg. 249	*Leymus condensatus* 'Canyon Prince'
Pink Honeysuckle pg. 255	*Lonicera hispidula*

ANNUAL WILDFLOWERS

Create your own super-bloom or color-accent patch with mass-planted annuals. Typically these readily reseed and create a long-lasting soil seed bank for a display every year. Sow seeds in late autumn for germination by winter rains.

COMMON NAME	SCIENTIFIC NAME
Baby Blue Eyes pg. 155	*Nemophila menziesii*
California Goldfields pg. 167	*Lasthenia californica*
California Poppy pg. 169	*Eschscholzia californica*
Chinese Houses pg. 175	*Collinsia heterophylla*
Common Madia pg. 181	*Madia elegans*
Common Sunflower pg. 183	*Helianthus annuus*
Farewell to Spring pg. 191	*Clarkia amoena*
Globe Gilia pg. 195	*Gilia capitata*
Meadowfoam pg. 207	*Limnanthes douglasii*
Tansy-Leaf Phacelia pg. 227	*Phacelia tanacetifolia*
Tidy Tips pg. 229	*Layia platyglossa*

Larval Host List (By Butterfly/Moth Species)

Plants marked with an asterisk (*) are not featured in this book.

BUTTERFLIES

Acmon Blue
(*Plebejus acmon*)

Buckwheats, pgs. 63, 117, 131, 179, 225
(*Eriogonum* spp.)

Lupines, pgs. 133, 159
(*Lupinus* spp.)

Black Swallowtail
(*Papilio polyxenes*)

Parsley family*
(Apiaceae)

California Dogface
(*Zerene eurydice*)

Southern Dogface
(*Zerene cesonia*)

False Indigo*
(*Amorpha fruticosa*)

Legume family, pgs. 51, 133, 159
(Fabaceae)

California Sister
(*Adelpha californica*)
Arizona Sister
(*Adelpha eulalia*)

Oaks*
(*Quercus* spp.)

California Tortoiseshell
(*Nymphalis californica*)

California Lilacs, pgs, 55, 69, 151
(*Ceanothus* spp.)

Checkered White
(*Pontia protodice*)

Bladderpod*
(*Peritoma arborea*)

Mustard family*
(Brassicaceae)

Common Buckeye
(*Junonia coenia*)

Penstemons, pgs. 193, 215
(*Penstemon* spp.)

Plantain family, pgs. 103, 111, 175, 193, 215
(Plantaginaceae)

Common Checkered-Skipper
(*Pyrgus communis*)

Mallow family, pgs. 67, 79, 115, 173
(Malvaceae)

Echo Azure
(*Celastrina echo*)

Blackberries*
(*Rubus* spp.)

California Buckeye, pg. 43
(*Aesculus californica*)

California Lilacs, pgs, 55, 69, 151
(*Ceanothus* spp.)

Edith's Checkerspot
(*Euphydryas editha*)

Chinese Houses, pg. 175
(*Collinsia heterophylla*)

Owl's Clover*
(*Orthocarpus* spp.)

Penstemons, pgs. 193, 215
(*Penstemon* spp.)

Funereal Duskywing
(*Erynnis funeralis*)

Baby Blue Eyes, pg. 155
(*Nemophila menziesii*)

Legume family, pgs. 51,
133, 159
(Fabaceae)

Gray Hairstreak
(*Strymon melinus*)

Buckwheats, pgs. 63, 117, 131,
179, 225
(*Eriogonum* spp.)

Chamise, pg. 75
(*Adenostoma fasciculatum*)

Legume family, pgs. 51,
133, 159
(Fabaceae)

Mallow family, pgs. 67, 79,
115, 173
(Malvaceae)

Gulf Fritillary
(*Agraulis vanillae*)

Passion Vine*
(*Passiflora* spp.)

Monarch, Queen
(*Danaus plexippus, D. gilippus*)

Milkweeds, pgs. 209, 221
(*Asclepias* spp.)

Mourning Cloak
(*Nymphalis antiopa*)

Cottonwoods & Aspens*
(*Populus* spp.)

Elm*
(*Ulmus* spp.)

Willows*
(*Salix* spp.)

Painted Lady
(*Vanessa cardui*)

Common Sunflower, pg. 183
(*Helianthus annuus*)

Globemallow*
(*Sphaeralcea* spp.)

Legume family, pgs. 51,
133, 159
(Fabaceae)

Thistles*
(*Cirsium* spp.)

Western Pearly Everlasting,
pg. 231
(*Anaphalis margaritacea*)

Yarrow, pg. 235
(*Achillea millefolium*)

Pipevine Swallowtail
(*Battus philenor*)

California Dutchman's Pipe,
pg. 243
(*Aristolochia californica*)

Reakirt's Blue
(*Echinargus isola*)

Legume family, pgs. 51,
133, 159
(Fabaceae)

BUTTERFLIES (continued)

Two-Tailed Swallowtail
(*Papilio multicaudata*)

Chokecherry, pg. 81
(*Prunus virginiana*)

Western Hop Tree*
(*Ptelea crenulata*)

Velvet Ash*
(*Fraxinus velutina*)

Variable (Chalcedon) Checkerspot
(*Euphydryas chalcedona*)

Common Snowberry, pg. 85
(*Symphoricarpos albus*)

Honeysuckles, pg. 139, 255
(*Lonicera* spp.)

Penstemons, pgs. 193, 215
(*Penstemon* spp.)

Variegated Fritillary
(*Euptoieta claudia*)

Flax*
(*Linum* spp.)

Passion Vine*
(*Passiflora* spp.)

Purslane*
(*Portulaca* spp.)

Violets, pg. 165
(*Viola* spp.)

Western Tiger Swallowtail
(*Papilio rutulus*)

Hollyleaf Cherry, p. 45
(*Prunus ilicifolia* ssp. *ilicifolia*)

Cottonwoods & Aspens*
(*Populus* spp.)

Velvet Ash*
(*Fraxinus velutina*)

Willows*
(*Salix* spp.)

MOTHS

Ceanothus Silkmoth
(*Hyalophora euryalus*)

Buckthorns, pgs. 55, 65, 69, 151
(Rhamnaceae family)

Currants & Gooseberries, pgs, 77, 95, 99, 125
(*Ribes* spp.)

Manzanitas, pgs. 91, 105
(*Arctostaphylos* spp.)

Pacific Madrone, pg. 47
(*Arbutus menziesii*)

Five-Spotted Hawk Moth
(*Manduca quinquemaculata*)

Blue Witches, pg. 57
(*Solanum xanti*)

Pink Honeysuckle, pg. 255
(*Lonicera hispidula*)

Tiger Moth
(*Pyrrharctia isabella*)

Coast Aster, pg. 177
(*Symphyotrichum chilense*)

Common Sunflower, pg. 183
(*Helianthus annuus*)

White-Lined Sphinx Moth
(*Hyles lineata*)

Blue Witches, pgs. 57
(*Solanum xanti*)

Evening Primroses, pgs. 199
(*Oenothera* spp.)

Sacred Datura, pg. 213
(*Datura wrightii*)

Retail Sources of Northern California Native Seeds & Plants

Numerous nurseries in the region sell native plants, as do many public arboretums, botanical gardens, parks, and conservation areas. A curated list follows; call or check online for operating hours and ordering information. For a list of sources statewide, see www.calscape.org/nurseries.php.

Annie's Annuals & Perennials
www.anniesannuals.com

740 Market Avenue
Richmond, CA 94801
(510) 215-3301

Bay Natives
www.baynatives.com

10 Cargo Way
San Francisco, CA 94121
(415) 278-6755

Blossom Hill California Native Plants
www.blossomhillnatives.com
email: blossomhillnatives@gmail.com

Open by appointment only
Orange Blossom Road
Oakdale, CA
(209) 318-9011

Blue Moon Native Garden and Nursery
Plant list updated monthly, go to
www.bluemoonnative.com\ for information

Open by appointment only, email at
info@bluemoonnative.com
Carmel Valley 93924
(831) 659-1990

California Flora Nursery
www.calfloranursery.com

2990 Somers Street
Fulton, CA 95439
(707) 528-8813

Central Coast Wilds
www.centralcoastwilds.com

336-A Golf Club Drive
Santa Cruz, CA 95060
(831) 459-0655

Floral Native Nursery
www.floralnativenursery.com

14388 Meridian Road
Chico, CA 95973
(530) 892-2511

**Friends of Sausal Creek
Native Plant Nursery**
www.sausalcreek.org/native-plant-nursery
email: nursery@sausalcreek.org

Joaquin Miller Community Center
3594 Sanborn Drive
Oakland, CA 94602
(510) 325-9006

Golden Valley Nursery
www.goldenvalleynursery.com/california-natives
email: info@goldenvalleynursery.com

26701 South Lammers Road
Tracy, CA 95377
(209) 830-9200

Intermountain Nursery
www.intermountainnursery.com/nativeplants
email: grow@intermountainnursery.com

30443 North Auberry Road
Prather, CA 93651
(559) 855-3113

Las Pilitas Nursery
www.laspilitas.com

3232 Las Pilitas Road
Santa Margarita, CA 93453
(805) 438-5992

Linda Vista Native Plants
www.lindavistanatives.com
email: info@lindavistanatives.com

Online orders only
Saratoga, CA
(408) 216-3874

McConnell Arboretum & Garden Nursery,
www.turtlebay.org/gardens

Turtle Bay Exploration Park
1100 Arboretum Drive
Redding, CA 96003
(530) 242-3169

**Mendocino Coast
Botanical Gardens Nursery**
www.gardenbythesea.org/visit/retail-nursery
email: nursery@gardenbythesea.org

18220 North CA 1
Fort Bragg, CA 95437
(707) 964-4352

Mission Blue Nursery
www.mountainwatch.org/missionbluenursery
email: nursery@mountainwatch.org

3435 Bayshore Boulevard
Brisbane, CA 94005
(415) 467-6631

Mostly Natives Nursery
www.mostlynatives.com
email: info@mostlynatives.com

54 B Street, Unit D
Point Reyes Station, CA 94956
(415) 663-8835

Native Here Nursery
www.nativeherenursery.org

Tilden Regional Park
101 Golf Course Drive
Berkeley, CA 94708
(510) 549-0211

Norrie's Gift & Garden Shop
arboretum.ucsc.edu/shop
email: arboretum@ucsc.edu

UC Santa Cruz Arboretum
1156 High Street
Santa Cruz, CA 95064
(831) 502-2998

O'Donnells Fairfax Nursery
www.odonnellsnursery.com
email: info@odonnellsnursery.com

1700 Sir Francis Drake Boulevard
Fairfax, CA 94930
(415) 453-0372

Our City Community Nursery
www.ourcityforest.org/nursery
email: treenursery@ourcityforest.org

1000 Spring Street
San Jose, CA 95110
(408) 785-2302

Sierra Azul Nursery & Gardens
www.sierraazul.com
email: plants@sierraazul.com

2660 East Lake Avenue (CA 152)
Watsonville, CA 95076
(831) 728-2532

Sutro Native Plant Nursery
www.sutrostewards.org/nursery
email: info@sutrostewards.org

476 Johnstone Drive
San Francisco, CA 94131 (*no phone*)

UC Botanical Garden at Berkeley
botanicalgarden.berkeley.edu/shop-deck
email: gardenshop@berkeley.edu

200 Centennial Drive
Berkeley, CA 94720
(510) 642-3343

Watershed Nursery
www.watershednursery.com
email: sales@thewatershednursery.com

601-A Canal Boulevard
Richmond, CA 94804
(510) 234-2222

Villager Nursery
www.villagernursery.com
email: info@villegernursery.com

Varney/McIver Dairy House
10678 Donner Pass Road
Truckee, CA
(530) 587-0771

Yerba Buena Nursery
www.yerbabuenanursery.com
email: kathy@nativeplants.com

12511 San Mateo Road (CA 92)
Half Moon Bay, CA
(650) 851-1668

California Native Plant Society

www.cnps.org, (916) 447-2677

CNPS Chapters map: www.cnps.org/chapters/map

The California Native Plant Society (CNPS) is a nonprofit organization dedicated to the conservation of California native plants and their natural habitats, and to increasing the understanding, appreciation, and horticultural use of native plants. Thirty-five chapters across the state locally promote the CNPS's mission.

NORTHERN CALIFORNIA CHAPTERS

Bay Area

East Bay Chapter: www.ebcnps.org

Marin Chapter: www.cnpsmarin.org

Santa Clara Valley Chapter: www.cnps-scv.org

Willis Linn Jepson Chapter (Solano): jepson.cnps.org

Yerba Buena Chapter: www.cnps-yerbabuena.org

Central Coast

Monterey Bay Chapter: chapters.cnps.org/montereybay

San Luis Obispo Chapter: www.cnpsslo.org

Santa Cruz Chapter: www.cruzcnps.org

Foothills and Mountains

El Dorado County Chapter: www.eldoradocnps.org

Mount Lassen Chapter (Chico): mountlassen.cnps.org

Redbud Chapter (Placer and Nevada Counties): chapters.cnps.org/redbud

Shasta Chapter (Redding): www.shastacnps.org

Sierra Foothills Chapter (Amador, Calaveras, Mariposa, and Tuolumne Counties): www.sierrafoothillscnps.org

North Coast and Wine Country

Mendocino County Chapter: www.dkycnps.org

Milo Baker Chapter (Santa Rosa): milobaker.cnps.org

Napa Valley Chapter: chapters.cnps.org/napa

North Coast Chapter: www.northcoastcnps.org

Sanhedrin Chapter (Lake County and Inland Mendocino County): sanhedrin.cnps.org

Valley

Alta Peak Chapter (Tulare County): www.altapeakcnps.org

Kern County Chapter: kern.cnps.org

North San Joaquin Valley Chapter: nsj.cnps.org

Sacramento Valley Chapter: www.sacvalleycnps.org

Sequoia Chapter (Madera, Fresno, and Kings Counties): www.cnps-sequoia.org

Botanical Gardens & Arboretums

Clovis Botanical Garden
www.clovisbotanicalgarden.org

Open Wednesday–Sunday, 9 a.m.–4 p.m.;
closed Monday, Tuesday, and select holidays
945 North Clovis Avenue
Clovis, CA 93611
559-298-3091

Forrest Deaner Native Plant Botanic Garden
jepson.cnps.org/garden
parks.ca.gov/?page_id=476

Open daily, 8 a.m.–sunset
Benicia State Recreation Area
1 State Park Road
Benicia, CA 94510
(707) 648-1911

Humboldt Botanical Garden
www.hbgf.org

Open Wednesday–Sunday, 10 a.m.–5 p.m.
7707 Tompkins Hill Road
Eureka, CA 95503
(707) 442-5139

McConnell Arboretum & Botanical Gardens
www.turtlebay.org

Open daily, 7 a.m.–sunset
Turtle Bay Exploration Park
844 Sundial Bridge Drive
Redding, CA 96003
(530) 243-8850

McConnell Arboretum & Garden Nursery
www.turtlebay.org/gardens

Open daily, 7 a.m.–sunset
Turtle Bay Exploration Park
1100 Arboretum Drive
Redding, CA 96003
(530) 242-3169

Mendocino Coast Botanic Gardens
www.gardenbythesea.org

Open daily, 10 a.m.–5 p.m.;
reservations required
18220 CA 1
Fort Bragg, CA 95437
(707) 964-4352

Golden Gate National Parks Conservancy
www.parksconservancy.org
/conservation/native-plants

For information about a specific park,
check www.parksconservancy.org
/find-your-park.
(415) 561-3000

Nipomo Native Garden
www.nipomonativegarden.org
email: info@nipomonativegarden.org

Open daily, sunrise–sunset
Nipomo Regional Park
Osage Street at Camino Caballo
Nipomo, CA 93444 (*no phone*)

Regional Parks Botanic Garden
www.nativeplants.org

Open daily, 8:30 a.m.–5:30 p.m.
Tilden Regional Park
Wildcat Canyon Road
Berkeley, CA 94708
(510) 544-3169

San Luis Obispo Botanical Garden
www.slobg.org
email: info@slobg.org

Open daily, sunrise–sunset
3450 Dairy Creek Road
San Luis Obispo, CA 93405
(805) 541-1400

San Francisco Botanical Garden
www.sfbotanicalgarden.org

Open daily, 7:30 a.m.–6 p.m.
Golden Gate Park
1199 Ninth Avenue
San Francisco, CA 94122
(415) 661-1316

The Santa Barbara Botanic Garden
www.sbbg.org

Open daily, 10 a.m.–6 p.m.
1212 Mission Canyon Road
Santa Barbara, CA 93105
(805) 682-4726

UC Botanical Garden at Berkeley
botanicalgarden.berkeley.edu

*Open daily, 11 a.m.–5 p.m.;
reservations required*
200 Centennial Drive
Berkeley, CA 94720
(510) 643-2755

UC Davis Arboretum and Public Garden
arboretum.ucdavis.edu

Open 24-7 year-round
Valley Oak Cottage
448 La Rue Road
Davis, CA 95616
(530) 752-4880

UC Santa Cruz Arboretum & Botanic Garden
arboretum.ucsc.edu
email: arboretum@ucsc.edu

Open daily, 9 a.m.–5 p.m.
1156 High Street
Santa Cruz, CA
(831) 502-2998

Index

Photo Credits

Interior photos by George Oxford Miller except as noted below. All photos copyright of their respective photographers.

Carole Price: 280

These images are licensed under the CC0 1.0 Universal (CC0 1.0) Public Domain Dedication license, which is available at https://creativecommons.org/publicdomain/zero/1.0/ or licensed under Public Domain Mark 1.0, which is available at https://creativecommons.org/publicdomain/mark/1.0/: **ALAN SCHMIERER:** 57, 95, 103, 201, 258; **Alex:** 117, 268 (California Dogface butterfly), 268 (California Sister butterfly); **Alex Heyman:** 174; **deedesie:** 231; **Irene:** 175; **Jesse Rorabaugh:** 268 (Echo Azure larva); **Marcus Tamura:** 269 (Edith's Checkerspot larva); **peter-f:** 270 (Ceanothus silkmoth larva); **Robb Hannawacker:** 268 (Checkered White larva)

These images are licensed under the Attribution 2.0 Generic (CC BY 2.0) license, which is available at https://creativecommons.org/licenses/by/2.0/: **Belinda Lo, Pacific Southwest Forest Service, USDA:** 171, no modifications, original image at https://www.flickr.com/photos/usfsregion5/26967399827/; **B Smith:** 269 (Gray Hairstreak larva), no modifications, original image at https://www.flickr.com/photos/twiztedminds/50355917511/; **chuck b.:** 59, no modifications, original image at https://www.flickr.com/photos/82479320@N00/7315542048/; **Colin Durfee:** 245, no modifications, original image at https://www.flickr.com/photos/146003125@N02/49911191453/; **JKehoe_Photos:** 99, no modifications, original image at https://www.flickr.com/photos/johnjkehoe_photography/12258968084/; **Nature-Shutterbug:** 241, no modifications, original image at https://www.flickr.com/photos/deinandra/3457457413/; **Peter Stevens:** 233, no modifications, original image at https://www.flickr.com/photos/nordique/5921241888/; **Stephanie Falzone, Plant Right:** 252, no modifications, original image at https://www.flickr.com/photos/149372353@N02/41260888694/; **Steve Jurvetson:** 21 (moth #6), no modifications, original image at https://commons.wikimedia.org/wiki/File:Pyrrharctia_isabella.jpg; **Tom Brandt:** 146, no modifications, original image at https://www.flickr.com/photos/12567713@N00/7380084566/; **Tom Hilton:** 192, no modifications, original image at https://www.flickr.com/photos/tomhilton/5722386925/

These images are licensed under the Attribution 4.0 International (CC BY 4.0) license, which is available at https://creativecommons.org/licenses/by/4.0/:

Alan Rockefeller: 145, no modifications, original image at https://www.inaturalist.org/photos/8117853; **barbarab:** 90, no modifications, original image at https://www.inaturalist.org/photos/30769129; **Ben Keen:** 270 (Tiger Moth), no modifications, original image at https://www.inaturalist.org/photos/133253179; **Casey H. Richart:** 75, no modifications, original image at https://www.inaturalist.org/photos/127528533; **Daniel:** 79, no modifications, original image at https://www.inaturalist.org/photos/135886244, 149, no modifications, original image at https://www.inaturalist.org/photos/123948872, 249, no modifications, original image at https://www.inaturalist.org/photos/122896685; **Don Loarie:** 191, no modifications, original image at http://www.flickr.com/photos/57556735@N08/7199106874, 211, no modifications, original image at http://www.flickr.com/photos/57556735@N08/5829840633, 268 (California tortoiseshell larva), no modifications, original image at https://www.inaturalist.org/photos/122111029; **Gail:** 49, no modifications, original image at https://www.inaturalist.org/photos/73451799; **George Williams:** 181, no modifications, original image at https://www.inaturalist.org/photos/79208889; **icosahedron:** 87, no modifications, original image at https://www.inaturalist.org/photos/168246117; **joergmlpts:** 131, no modifications, original image at https://www.inaturalist.org/photos/101266373; **John A Haskins:** 129, no modifications, original image at https://www.inaturalist.org/photos/102783051; **Julia Wittmann:** 253, no modifications, original image at https://www.inaturalist.org/photos/172261371; **Karen and Mike:** 141, no modifications, original image at https://www.inaturalist.org/photos/38291148; **Ken-ichi Ueda:** 268 (California Sister larva), no modifications, original image at https://www.inaturalist.org/photos/22178281; **Matt D'Agrosa:** 270 (Chalcedon Checkerspot larva), no modifications, original image at https://www.inaturalist.org/photos/30738866; **Ryan Elliott:** 205, no modifications, original image at https://www.inaturalist.org/photos/26835908; **Sula Vanderplank:** 73, no modifications, original image at https://www.inaturalist.org/photos/42917741, 111, no modifications, original image at https://www.inaturalist.org/photos/37678421

Images used under license from shutterstock.com.

Akash Lanjekar: 269 (Queen larva); **avkost:** 85; **Bankiras:** 226; **brajianni:** 210; **Brian B Fox:** 14; **Christine Stafford:** 270 (Two-tailed Swallowtail larva); **DailyGarden:** 97; **Danita Delimont:** 51, 262 inset; **David Byron Keener:** 269 (Funereal duskywing butterfly); **Debra Bernal:** 270 (Chalcedon Checkerspot butterfly); **Debu55y:** 207; **Dee Carpenter Originals:** 81; **delobol:** 84; **Dmitry Fch:** 269 (Painted Lady larva); **Dominic Gentilcore PhD:** 215; **Dreamers Lil Dream Shoppe:** 165; **Elvira Werkman:** 55; **Fabian Junge:** 147; **Gardens by Design:** 10; **goran cakmazovic:** 15, moth syndrome; **grandbrothers:** 164; **Greens and Blues:** 244; **Gurcharan Singh:** 86, 110; **inimma:** 247; **Jacob Hamblin:** 270 (Western Tiger Swallowtail larva); **James Lesser:** 151; **Jayne Gulbrand:** 157; **Jeff Huth:** 268 (California tortoiseshell butterfly); **Jennifer Bosvert:** 125; **Judy M Darby:** 268 (Common Buckeye larva); **Kamrad71:** 230; **karamysh:** 46; **Karpova Natalia:** 257; **K E Magoon:** 69; **Keneva Photography:** title page; **kzww:** 19, bumble bee inset; **Le Do:** 20, monarch inset; **Ienic:** 54, 68; **LianeM:** 206; **Lu Lovelock:** 195; **Marygdobson:** 148; **Massimiliano Paolino:** 269 (Mourning Cloak larva); **melissamn:** 96; **Michael G McKinne:** 270 (Variegated Fritillary butterfly); **Nahhana:** 58; **Nancy Bauer:** 235; **Nikki Yancey:** 143; **OlenaSA:** 133; **OlgaOtto:** 124; **OpsimathPhotography:** 107; **Patrick Poendl:** 120; **photosgenius:** 109; **Pieter Bruin:** 113; **Praphaporn Anontachai:** 155; **Rabbitti:** 221; **Robert Lessmann:** 227; **Ruth Swan:** 47; **Sari ONeal:** 270 (Variegated Fritillary larva), 270 (Five-spotted Hawkmoth butterfly); **Sean Xu:** 223; **ShutterstockProfessional:** 105; **Simone Hogan:** 11; **Slawinka:** 123; **South12th Photography:** 193; **Stefan Schug:** 139; **SvetlanaSF:** 12; **Steve JM Hamilton:** 88; **Sundry Photography:** 40, 43, 56, 63, 66, 74, 77, 82, 83, 91, 115, 135, 136, 140, 159, 160, 166, 167, 169, 170, 180, 185, 197, 200, 228, 229, 256, 269 (Edith's Checkerspot butterfly); **SunflowerMomma:** 214; **Thani Normai:** 154; **Tikhomirov Sergey:** 219; **Todd Aaron Sanchez:** 6; **Tony Baggett:** 188; **Tom Meaker:** 127; **Tonya Koreneva:** 50; **vebboy:** 150; **Vladimir Staykov:** 39; **yhelfman:** 137, 187

About the Author

George Oxford Miller is a botanist, nature photographer, environmental journalist, and near-lifelong resident of the West. He has lived in California, Texas, and Arizona, and he now resides in New Mexico. He is a longtime member of the Native Plant Society of California and is past president of the Albuquerque chapter of the Native Plant Society of New Mexico. George holds a master's degree in zoology and botany from the University of Texas at Austin. He has also written five wildflower mobile apps and 23 nature guidebooks. George's books for Adventure Publications include *Native Plant Gardening for Birds, Bees & Butterflies: Southern California,* two Wildflower Quick Guides to Southern and Northern California, and *Backyard Science & Discovery Workbook: California.* His web magazine, TravelsDuJour.com, is dedicated to environmental conservation and sustainable nature tourism.